Merci Beaucoup

A Story of
Courage and Compassion

Convent of Mercy

Kinsale 1844 - 2002

Johanna O'Mahony Walters

Published by:

Johanna O'Mahony Walters

Church House

Steynton

Milford Haven

Pembrokeshire.

Sponsors:

Sisters of Mercy, Southern Region

Bank of Ireland, South Mall, Cork

Allied Irish Bank, Kinsale

ISBN: 0-9541849-0-4

Printed by Bandon Printers Ltd. Tel: 023 41704

Acknowledgements

A big "Thank You" to the many wonderful people without whose help and support this book would never have come to birth. Firstly Sr.Clare McCarthy who had the idea and to the two "Angels of Mercy" Sr.Immaculata Hourihane and Sr.Patricia Quinlan who have walked every step of the way from conception to birth with this book.

The many contributors who generously gave their time to write their tributes and memories all of which beautifully enhance the work:

Babs Collins

Sr.Finbarr Morrissey

Sr.Carmel Collins

Mary Aherne Thompson

Sr.Benignus Cremins

Sr.Eleanor O'Leary

Niamh McEvoy

Sr.Clare McCarthy

Sr.Kevin O'Brien

Sr.Mary O'Donovan

Eugene Gillan

Vera O'Herlihy

Rosie Cargin

Pat Holohan

Sr.Elma Coakley

Christie Fitzgerald

Sr.Agnes Beary

Michael Cronin

Sr.Yvonne Collins

Sr.Joesph Keohane

Pat Crowley

Sr.Clare Fennell

Sr.Mary McAuliffe

Sr.Gabriel Sweeney

Sr.Patricia Quinlan

Fr.Myles McSweeney

Sr.Mary O'Donoghue

Donal McDonnell

Alex Archer

Mary Cooper

Louise Tobin

Catherine Duggan

Sr.Josephine Keohane

Special thanks to Alice Taylor for agreeing to write the forward.

Thanks to the following Archivists who have been so patient and helpful with my many queries.

Sr. Agnes Gleeson	Mercy International Centre Baggot St.Dublin
Sr.Marilyn Gouailhardou	Sisters of Mercy Burlingame, California
Sr.Stanislaus	Convent of Mercy, Clonakilty
Sr.Gertrude Cannon	Convent of Mercy Ballyshannon
Sr.Mary Berding	Regional Community of Cincinnati
Sr.Evelyn Kenny	Convent of Mercy,Newry
Sr.Angela Bugler	St.Mary's Convent of Mercy Limerick
Sr.Barbara Jeffrey	Mercy Institute, Birmingham
Sr. Peter and Sr. Francesco	Convent of Mercy, Macroom, Co. Cork

Thanks to the photographers: Thanks to those who loaned photographs:

Sr.Patricia Quinlan	Sr.Agnes Beary
Sr.Eleanor O'Leary	Sr.Immaculata Hourihane
Sr.Eileen McSweeney	Sr.Patricia Quinlan
David Walters	Philomena Hurley

Thanks to John Booth, my computer guru for his help and advice.

Line Drawing of Convent:	Patrica Lordan
The Maps:	Marilyn Lawrie
Navigation advice:	Ken Watson.
Layout Advice:	Mike Donovan

Thanks to Central Bank for permission to reproduce the £5.

Editors and Readers thanks for your help with the text:

Sr.Eleanor O'Leary	Sr.Gabriel Sweeney
Sr.Immaculata Hourihane	Sr.Patricia Quinlan
Sr.Jacqui Moore	Steve Latham
	Marilyn Lawrie

Thanks for all the "running about"

Sr.Mary McAuliffe   Sr.Clare McCarthy

                                            Norma Deasy

Thanks to Sr.Joan and Community, Kinsale for making me so welcome during my two periods of research.

Thanks to David and Neil for their love and support during this project.

Lastly thanks to Robert Merrick and his team at Bandon Printers for the kindness, sensitivity and professionalism they have shown during this project.

The Open Door
Symbol of Mercy Hospitality

*I dedicate this book to all those brave Sisters
who passed through this door during its 157 - year history
and especially to those who will walk through it
for the last time in 2002.*

The Works of Mercy

Feed the Hungry
Give drink to the thirsty
Clothe the naked
Visit the sick
Visit the imprisoned
Shelter the homeless
Bury the dead

Instruct the Ignorant
Counsel the doubtful
Comfort the Sorrowful
Convert the sinner
Bear wrongs patiently
Forgive injury
Pray for the living and the Dead.

Contents

Preface
A Timely Tribute.

Nuns are an endangered species. A cry of protest would wake the mighty heavens if the same were to happen in the animal kingdom. In Ireland farming methods have been modified in some areas to preserve the Corncrake. It had limited success. Does this prove as the bible states that there is a season for everything? Has the time for nuns gone? Or is it that our world vulgarised by excess has become unappreciative of what they have to offer. Is there in human nature a tendency to kill the things we love? Though not everyone loved the nuns and maybe those who had reason not to love them are more vocal than those who remember them with respect.

Is there in us humans an inclination to "bring down the noble stag". Will future generations look back in disbelieving amazement at these heroic women who sacrificed so much for the love of God and the common good? Will they find it difficult to understand our lack of appreciation and how casually and insensitively these nuns were replaced?

Maybe some nuns like many others lost sight of their original high ideals but without most of these women the uneducated of Ireland would have remained the uneducated and many orphans would have died in the gutter. Maybe today there is a tendency to judge past generations with today's social conscience but who are we to sit in judgement? When you look at today's homeless we must admit that even with our increased wealth and facilities we are not doing such a great job. Now, we are much more image conscious, better at making things look good, our window dressing is better than that of past generations.

When we look back we are very critical of the unpaid social workers of the past, namely the nuns. In private many people remember them gratefully but publicly in recent years they have got very bad press. The mistakes of a few have tarnished the memory of many. This must be very difficult for the many dedicated Sisters who have given their lives to schools and hospitals not only in Ireland but all over the world.

This book is coming at the right time. It traces the history of the Mercy Order in Kinsale and because it is a historical record there is of necessity application to dates and details but darned through the pages is the appreciation of the ordinary people of Kinsale. The nuns came to them when times were hard and set up a school and a hospital and provided employment. Many of their past pupils remember them with love and respect. The nuns in their wisdom introduced the women of Kinsale to the delicate craft of lace making to provide a much-needed income. Though that craft has died there must be pieces of beautiful Kinsale lace treasured in many local homes. Is there any yardstick by which to judge the sense of elegance this beautiful lace brought to Kinsale.

I have a lovely little piece of Kinsale lace that I got many years ago from Fr.Michael O'Riordan who ministered in Kinsale and later came to my parish of Innishannon. At a recent first station Mass in my home it graced the altar and was much admired for its beauty and delicacy.

Their lace is a relic of these gifted women who came to Kinsale to grace the lives of its people and left a legacy of education and caring. We need to be publicly reminded of the debt of gratitude that is owed to these nuns. In this book Kinsale through the pen of Joan O'Mahony Walters has done just that. It is a fitting tribute to wonderful women who moulded the soul of this beautiful town.

Alice Taylor.

Introduction

Writing this book has for me, been a Sacred Trust. I lived almost ten years of my life as a member of the Mercy Community, Kinsale, a part of my history of which I am very proud. The names of Mother Mary Ann Burke and Mother Francis Bridgemen are as familiar to me as those of my own grandparents; they are part of my heritage. Telling the stories of Sisters whose names I had heard spoken with awe has been a challenge and a privilege. Through my research I have been in contact with the descendants of these Sisters, other dedicated women who are still inspired by the vision and courage of women like Mother Joseph Lynch or Mother Baptist Russell. The stories of the leaders of the various foundations have been documented in this book but let us also remember the Sisters who accompanied them, who made it possible for them to accomplish "great things" by their own dedication and hard work.

There is one glaring gap in the book, which is a cause of personal sadness to me, as I know it is to the Sisters at St.Joseph's. It is the story of the many orphans who lived their lives in the Kinsale Convent and who are so much part of this story. I have first hand experience of the love with which these girls were loved. I have heard them being spoken of fondly and seen that they were corresponded with regularly. They were always referred to as "our own" and welcomed back to the Convent whenever they chose to come. The care taken of these children by Sr.Dympna, Sr.De Pazzi, Sr. Teresita, Sr.Assumpta and Sr.Lawrence to mention but a few is legendary. Their musical and artistic talents were encouraged and developed and when they went to work, I have been told that Sr.Dympna, like any good parent, saw to it that they were paid a just wage. No doubt there was discipline as there is in any good home, we have all in our own homes experienced a smack or a telling off and no doubt all of us as parents have had to discipline our own children. Before the 1960's the Victorian notion of children "being seen but not heard" was widespread, thankfully all that has changed and children now do have a voice.

The tributes paid to the Sisters by the many contributors to this work is a measure of their commitment to the education of the young people and the esteem in which they are held by former students and colleagues alike.

There is strong evidence that the Mercy Charism will continue to go from strength to strength in Kinsale, a town with a finely tuned social conscience. A town which has been fortunate in its Mercy role models.

BALLYSHANNON

NEWRY

IRELAND

DUBLIN

LIMERICK

DOON

CORK

RIVER BANDON KINSALE
BANDON
SKIBBEREEN
CLONAKILTY

Chapter 1
The First Century of Mercy

Kinsale, said to be one of Ireland's oldest towns, the oldest some would argue, has a unique and special place in Irish history since Ireland was first inhabited. Kinsale has clearly been an important settlement since the sixth century, even though it is not quite clear when it received its first charter. The town dates to its first "known" charter that of 1334.

Ceann Saile, the town at the head of the sea, has a wealth of spiritual presence since St.Eltin's time in the sixth century. St Eltin, or Multose, is of course the town's patron or even its founder. A Carmelite friary dedicated to the Blessed Virgin Mary was founded in 1334. The friars looked after the lepers near Browns Mills. During the Penal times the Carmelites had to go into hiding just outside the town at Ballintober. In Tracton, just seven miles from Kinsale, a Cistercian Abbey was founded in 1224. It being the daughter house of Whitland Abbey in West Wales the community was made up exclusively of English and Welsh monks.

Kinsale was an important garrison town during the British occupation. It played host to both King Charles 1st and King James 2nd! Subsequently it became an important fishing port.

When the Sisters of Mercy arrived in 1844 on the eve of the famine it had lost much of its former glory. The dockyard had closed. The bigger ships were using the larger harbour in Cork. The poor in Kinsale were experiencing difficult times.

The town's parish priest, young and dynamic Father Justin Foley McNamara, worked tirelessly for the poor of the town. He had a special concern for the girls and young women of the town who were uneducated and unemployed. He felt they were at risk from the young soldiers billeted in the local barracks.

When his young widowed sister, Mary Ann Burke, approached him to say she wished to use her considerable wealth to found a convent in her native Macroom, he persuaded her that Kinsale's need was much greater. She changed her mind and joined the Convent of Mercy in Limerick with a view to coming to Kinsale as a Sister of Mercy.

The heiress, Catherine McAuley, had founded the Mercy Order in Dublin on December 12th 1831. She is now of course the Venerable Catherine McAuley honoured by both Church and state, her picture appearing on the £5 note.

While his sister was completing her Novitiate in Limerick, Fr Justin was searching for a house for the Sisters in Kinsale. He eventually found a two-storey house and a plot of ground at the top of the hill, a place known as The Rampart, which he managed to buy with the money

Mary Anne had given him. He had her furniture and personal belongings moved in there, and her beautiful furniture and silver is still to be seen today in both parlours at the convent.

On April 19th 1844 the first Sisters arrived in Kinsale late in the afternoon. I am sure the locals found them a strange sight, in their simple dress and with few belongings, making their way with Fr.Justin towards their new home. The little group consisted of Mother Francis Bridgeman who was to be the Mother Superior and Mother Mary Anne Burke the Foundress of the Kinsale convent and Mother Assistant. Sister M.Xavier Barry and Sister Martha accompanied them. Rev. Mother Elizabeth Moore and Sister M de Sales Bridgeman of Limerick completed the little group. They stayed a month and helped establish the convent. The Bishop - Rev. Dr. Murphy of Cork - placed the Convent under the patronage of St.Joseph, and under the spiritual direction of Fr.Justin. Very little is known of the Sisters' early days in Kinsale. No doubt they were busy settling in and establishing their spiritual routine, changing the usage from an ordinary house to a convent. The house consisted of what are now the two convent parlours and three rooms of the infirmary.

While the Sisters were waiting for their own school to be built they attended and taught in the local National School at the Half Wall. This school had opened in 1837 as a school for boys, a school for girls being added later and housed on the first floor of the same building. This building has since being incorporated into the Convent Boarding School and Domestic Science Room.

The nuns immediately began the religious instruction of adults and children and the visitation of the old and the sick. There was tremendous poverty in Kinsale at that time and many of the people were ashamed to attend Mass because of their shabby clothes, but Mother Francis Bridgeman invited them to attend Mass at the Convent.

The foundation stone for the school and part of the convent was laid on July 2nd 1844, and the school opened its doors to seven hundred students on March 28th 1845 with only six Sisters to teach them! - Three professed Sisters, one novice and two postulants. These remarkable women did not let the grass grow under their feet. Neither did the builders who must have worked so very hard. By November they were admitting people for the house of Mercy and orphanage, which had not yet been built! Great was their Faith! In November they said good-bye to Sisters M.Xavier and Martha who were recalled to Limerick.

The town and convent of Kinsale suffered a very great loss when their beloved Fr.Justin died on December 31st '45 while taking a well-earned rest at Gibraltar. The people of Kinsale carried his coffin on their shoulders, all the way from Cork to John the Baptist Parish Church which he had built. There was such an outpouring of grief at his funeral that the Celebrant had to ask the people to restrain themselves so that he could continue with the funeral Mass. Mother Mary Anne had lost a dear brother, and Mother Francis lost her earthly support. The whole venture of establishing Mercy in Kinsale was now committed solely to God.

Part of original Convent

Front Parlour

First Infirmary, where Mass was celebrated

Back Parlour

Apostles Corridor

In September 1846 the foundation stone for the chapel was laid. By December of the same year the Sisters were serving dinners to the starving poor, even the bishop was lending a hand - cutting bread, etc. The Bishop of Hyderabad in India, who was the brother of the Bishop of Cork, gave money for the poor and was a great help to the sisters in establishing a soup kitchen at the convent. This gentleman seemed to have spent some time in the area during his brother's illness, because he deputised for him at the profession of Sr.M.Joseph Lynch, Kinsale's first postulant, whose extraordinary story you shall read later.

By early 1847 the famine was general throughout the country, the poor people were starving. With the help of donations from various friends, about six hundred children were fed twice daily in the school. They were given Indian meal, or yellow meal as it was called, rice and biscuits. Even with the many donations from individuals and groups, there was still not enough to feed everybody who was in such dire need.

The Sisters tried in many ways to bring relief: They rented a house for the training of poor people for domestic service. The Industrial school for girls was established. This became known as the "factory" because of the variety of work carried on there - various kinds of needlework, knitting, making artificial flowers, carding both hemp and wool.

Many countrywomen were employed spinning hemp into twine for the nets. The Rope Walk was lined on either side by trees, the fishing ropes were twined between the trees and when finished, they were - led by the local band - carried on the shoulders of the men to the Quay!

The community bought the materials to make the fishing nets in order to help the wives and daughters of fishermen. Even with all this "employment", several young girls were obliged to go to the workhouse.

At this time the Sisters taught Limerick lace, muslin embroidery and other kinds of work, which helped provide employment for the women and girls of the town. Rev Mother Francis Bridgeman went to Limerick to acquire some knowledge of lacemaking and to get the necessary materials to proceed with this venture. A qualified person from the National Board came to teach the Muslin Embroidery.

Cholera broke out in May 1849. The Sisters' help was offered for the hospital. The guardians of the Workhouse had permitted the nuns to nurse the patients by day on condition that they confine themselves to the "religious instruction of the Roman Catholic paupers" only, but when Asiatic Cholera broke out they were glad to have the Sisters there night and day. They worked in shifts from 6 A.M. to 7 P.M. and from 7 P.M. to 6 A.M. As there were only ten professed Sisters, the novices and postulants had to help also. One patient in particular benefited from this concession. Sr.Vincent, while attending to a poor woman brought in from the country, was called to another patient. On her return she was shocked to see the countrywoman's bed empty. She was told that the patient had died and had been taken to the mortuary, ready to be thrown into the Poll Buidhe, as the common grave was known. Sr. Vincent, hurried to the mortuary, held a small mirror to the mouth of the lady and found that she was still alive. She survived for another forty years!

In one week alone the number in the Workhouse and auxiliary wards totalled 2,240, including 150 fever patients and 164 who had contracted other diseases. One day 122 uncoffined corpses were just thrown into the Poll Buidhe.

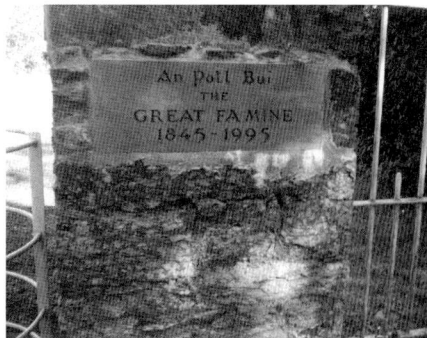

Site of Poll Buidhe

A local gentleman, Mr.Buckley, put his horse and cart at the disposal of the Sisters so they did not have to walk back and forth. Doctors and all those in charge in the hospital were very grateful for the Sisters' help. As a "reward" they were allowed to visit the Workhouse from which they had been previously banned. Six to eight Sisters visited the poor inmates weekly until September 8th 1893 when they took up residence there to nurse the patients. In August 1894, a chaplain was appointed, and Mass was celebrated in the Workhouse chapel - The times they were a- changing!

Apart from the Poor Servants of the Mother of God, the Sisters of Mercy were the only Religious Congregation to work in Workhouses in Ireland.

Convent Chapel from Organ Gallery

During this very difficult time in the history of our nation the little community at St.Joseph's grew steadily. In August 1849 the positions of Novice Mistress and Bursar were filled, Sister Teresa Maher becoming Novice Mistress while Sister Vincent Dignam became Bursar. The opening of the Convent Chapel to the public on February 24th 1850 was a truly wonderful occasion for the community and the townspeople. At Christmas that year, they had their first public crib in the chapel. Before the Christmas Mass clothes were distributed to the poor and to the needy children who were given Christmas dinner at the convent.

Christmas Crib in Convent Chapel

Religious Instruction for boys began on Sundays. Many men asked if they too could attend. Out of this humble beginning grew The Men's Society.

The Community experienced great sadness in 1852 with the first death of one of their number. Sister Magdalen, who died after a short illness, was only twenty-three years old. Although seven Sisters caught fever at that time, she was the only one who died.

With the outbreak of typhus fever in the town in 1853 the Sisters were once again extremely busy nursing the victims. Unfortunately, Sister Paul caught fever from one of the curates she was nursing and died just one year after her first profession.

1849 to 1867 was a time of great expansion for the little Community on the hill. Many postulants were received and there were annual receptions and professions. This enabled the community to respond to requests for Sisters to work in various missions. This expansion needs a chapter to itself - more later.

The work of the Sisters was appreciated by many who were in a position to help the needy of Kinsale. They had several benefactors ready to support their efforts. Mr P.Scannell, gave a pretty marble altar, an oil painting, and statues of Mary, St. Joseph and a Guardian Angel to furnish the Chapel of Mary. The M.P., Sir John Arnott, gave thirty-six pairs of blankets to the orphanage.

The school had the first of many successful inspections in 1861. It was found to be well run and efficient, with a high standard of education and care for the children. A grant of £20 was given for equipment - a princely sum in those days.

In 1862 the poor were still in great distress, due to the severe weather and the crop failure of the previous year. Children were still being fed at the convent. When they arrived in the mornings, they were given a warm bowl of stirabout for breakfast. Because of the great poverty and hardship being experienced by the people of the town, breakfast was given to all those in need. Sir John Arnott again showed his generosity by arranging to have four hundred loaves of bread delivered to the convent each week to help feed the hungry. Another benefactor, Sir G.Colthurst, gave £25 to be delivered as tickets for coal among the needy. Four hundred tickets were delivered.

Mr. Charles Kennedy gave £500 towards the building of a hospital to be attached to the Convent, under the patronage of St.Lawrence O'Toole. A site was duly chosen, but since the building of a hospital was not feasible at that time the money, plus some further donations, was used to build an Industrial School.

The Noviceship wing, called Nazareth, was built during 1865 - 1866. It was opened on June 8th1866 with a celebration of Mass and the profession of two Sisters. Mother Francis became Novice Mistress.

The Prayer Room, formerly the Noviceship

1865 was a significant year for the Sisters when water was piped into the convent and gas was used to light the chapel, choir, community room and kitchen. These innovations, no doubt, ended some of the drudgery and gave the Sisters more time for their caring work. In 1866 the Sisters took possession of the garden in front of the balcony.

The Convent Garden

1867 saw the Sisters collecting for a new orphanage. The collection being organised by local men: John Lordan, Thomas Buckley and Nicholas Walsh. The foundation stone of the new orphanage was laid in June. The late Mr. Cadogan of the Worlds End left a bequest of £115 towards the building, and the following year Mr.Charles Kennedy Junior gave a donation of £10.

In 1868 Mr Coward, Assistant Royal Commissioner, inspected the school and again a glowing report was received. He considered the children superior in intelligence and information to those of the same age in England!

The inspector of the Orphanage in 1869 was also well pleased with the whole establishment.

Mother Mary Anne Burke, foundress, and benefactress died in 1870 aged seventy-four.

This marked the end of an era for the young community, and it was with great sadness that they laid this gentle and humble lady to rest.

Amid great pomp and circumstance in 1872 the school played host to Earl and Countess Spencer, the vice regent of Ireland and his lady. They were both delighted with the reception they received and with the excellent behaviour and the entertainment provided by the children. They were loud in their praise of the Sisters and the children.

During this same year the Sisters received a visit from Mother M.Magdalen Taylor, a nursing friend from the Crimean days. Her name then was Fanny Taylor, daughter of an Anglican vicar. Through her friendship with the Sisters, particularly Mother Francis, she had converted to

Catholicism during her time in the East. On her return to London, she became the foundress of the Religious order known as "The Poor Servants of the Mother of God". Like the Mercy Order this order was devoted exclusively to the service or the poor.

In 1873 three of the beautiful stained glass windows which can still be seen in the chapel were purchased from Messrs Meyer and Co. of Munich at the cost of £100 each.

Father Dunlea was anxious that the Sisters should have an infant school for boys. To achieve his goal he gave a donation of £50 in 1874 toward the building of this school. Mr Collins M.P. for Kinsale at the time gave £100, Mr. Lordan £20, Fr.Kelleher P.P. of Kinsale, gave £10 and each curate gave £5. It was to be another four years before the building commenced and it was finally opened in August 1880. Over one hundred boys, all under six years of age, presented themselves on that first day.

Mother Francis published the first volume of her book -"God in His Works" in 1878. So in spite of all the services being provided by the Sisters and their huge building programme, they still had time to develop their own creativity.

During 1882 a group of Sisters left to work in the Workhouse at Youghal.

The beautiful set of Calvary figures, which are in the garden, and will be in the Sisters' cemetery on moving, were erected in 1883.

The Calvary in Convent Garden

Mr.A.Cole of the Science and Art Department of the South Kensington College, arrived in January 1884, with samples of lace which he had made in the lace making districts of Europe. Mr.Brennan, Head of the Cork School of Art, accompanied him. The object of the visit was to help the Kinsale lacemakers produce work which was equal to the foreign laces. Both men were very helpful and gave much useful advice.

A lot of improvements were made to the convent during 1884. Chapel and choir were painted in oils, the marble altars were erected and tiles were laid in the chapel and cloisters, these tiles are still there.

Lower Corridor - example of tiling

1885 saw considerable expansion. The community numbered fifty sisters, the first time since the foundation that the community was so large. As more space was needed it was decided to build new cells/rooms for the Sisters over the Immaculate Conception School. This is now known as the Sacred Heart Corridor - a wide and airy space. Since the schools were also expanding it was decided to raise two storeys over the Infant Girls' school.

Sacred Heart Corridor

By 1886 the community were again called upon to help out in another Workhouse. This time the Bishop of Cloyne invited the Sisters to take care of the Midleton Workhouse, where the conditions were not good. They stayed there for six years ministering to the patients.

1888 saw the death of Mother Francis Bridgeman who had led the community for so many years.

In April of the same year the lace makers of Kinsale proudly exhibited their work in the Cork School of Art, where it was much admired. One of the pupils received a prize, which was presented by Lady Bandon.

Sample of Kinsale Lace

Professor of Music, Herr Swertz, started a course of instruction in vocal and instrumental music, forming a choir with the Sisters.

In 1890 a man broke into the convent between midnight and one o'clock in the morning. Some of the Sisters were disturbed by the sound of a window opening on the flag passage. After some investigation they found a pair of heavy boots and a pair of trousers on the ground outside the back sacristy window which was open. The police were called and the search continued. The man was found in the rope -walk in his stocking feet and flannel drawers. The Sisters asked the police to allow the man to get dressed before they frog-marched him to the police station, but they refused and he had to go through the town in this state of undress! He was sentenced to three months' imprisonment.

The Presentation Brothers arrived in Kinsale in 1891 and took charge of the Boys' School on the resignation of Mr.Michael Twomey, who was overcome by grief at the death of his son.

The Sisters were invited in 1892 to take over the Workhouse Hospital, amid great Protestant opposition.

In 1891 Sr.Clare Keane died. Formerly Arabella Keane, daughter of James and Elizabeth, was born in London in 1829. She entered the convent in 1847 and was one of the group who went to the Crimea with Mother Francis. She was renowned for her outstanding holiness and devotion to duty. Her brother, Daniel Keane of Cork, gave a stained glass window of St.Clare in her memory. It was installed in 1892 at the back of the choir where it can still be seen.

Stain Glass window, to the memory of Sr. Clare Keane

I am pleased to report that it will be transferred to Winters Hill.

Lady Aberdeen who was making a tour of Ireland visited the convent in 1893. She was anxious to promote Irish Industry and was seeking a display of Irish handcraft to exhibit at the Chicago "World's Fair" the following year. This visit is well documented in "St. Joseph's Convent of Mercy, Kinsale" by the late Frank Hurley.

1894 was the Jubilee year of the founding of the Convent. A new marble altar rail was erected in the chapel to mark the occasion. April 19th, the actual Jubilee day, was declared a holiday. A Pontifical High Mass was celebrated at eleven o'clock. The celebrant wore a beautiful new lace alb, which had been made by the lace workers in the workroom especially for this joyful occasion. The altars were radiant with lights and flowers. The Sisters visited the cemetery and decorated the graves of Mother Mary Anne Burke and Mother Francis Bridgeman. The celebrations continued for a few days and gifts were received from all the foundations, as well as a beautiful set of vestments from the motherhouse in Limerick. At that time the community consisted of fifty-nine sisters.

That same year a chaplain was appointed to the Workhouse so Mass was celebrated there daily.

The Resume of the year's activities for that Jubilee year reads as follows:

"Schools sustain good character. Extern schools attended by 400/500 pupils. Because parents are so poor they keep children from school as soon as they can, so they can go and earn a living. The sisters have employed some of the girls in the workroom Industrial Department. The lace making and other industries carried out there have received new impetus from the patronage of the Irish Industries Association.

The art class is a huge help to the lace making. Drawing is taught in all classes from the Infants upwards. Domestic Economy, Practical Cookery, Scientific Dressmaking, Sewing Machine, Fancy needlework, book keeping and vocal music (tonic solfa) are taught throughout the school.

There are large classes for the Sacraments. The Infant boys' school is well attended.

Industrial School (Orphans)

There are one hundred and fifty children of various ages, who receive training in domestic and literary skills. When sixteen they either go home to their friends or suitable situations are found for them. Those with special talent for drawing attend the art class.

Cecilia Keyes suffered illness and was encouraged to devote her time and attention to drawing. She soon developed a remarkable talent, and has become so good, she has won various prizes and certificates. She was the first to receive a Scholarship in 1892 and was appointed art Pupil-Teacher.

Some of the children show great talent and skill in lace work. Many of them are beautiful singers.

Most former pupils live good lives in many parts of the world. Some have preferred to stay on here as mistresses. Others have become nuns in France, America and elsewhere.

Visitation of the Sick: Clothing, fuel etc. is regularly distributed to the poor.

Wages: A large sum is paid out weekly in wages to work girls, extra teachers, janitors, tradesmen, etc.

There is a great improvement in the girls' school. We want it to be as like the Industrial school as possible. One of our former Industrial school children is engaged as assistant mistress and paid by the community, another is employed to help "mind" the younger children. The children's dress has been changed over the years to something resembling a uniform. The children and their surroundings here won the praise of inspectors over the years.

Hospital: Each ward has accommodation for sixty patients and each bed is occupied."

(Taken from the archives of the Convent of Mercy Kinsale.)

During 1895 two pupils, Albina Collins and Cecilia Keyes, received scholarships. Albina got a three-year scholarship to London. She also got a job as governess, which enabled her to live comfortably while in London. Cecilia obtained the benefit of a Vacation Course at South Kensington.

Tragedy struck Kinsale in 1896, when a big fire broke out in Market Street. Six large houses were completely destroyed - thankfully no lives were lost. The children were given a half day from school as a result.

An extension to the Industrial School was begun in 1897.

1898 saw the deaths of two of Kinsale's pioneering Sisters - Sr.Joseph Lynch died in Oregon, and Mother Baptist Russell died in San Francisco.

There were eighty workers engaged in lace making in 1899. Orders were coming in from many important people. A letter came from Windsor castle with a payment of £5 and ten shillings for a baby's robe which had been beautifully made in the workroom.

Lady Iveagh planned taking some of the work to the Paris Exhibition.

Early in 1905 the Sisters withdrew from the Youghal workhouse amid great sadness. They had spent twenty-three years there. The crowds flocked to say good-bye to them. Their place there was taken by "The Poor Servants of the Mother of God" - the order founded by their friend Fanny Taylor.

The Kinsale lace continued to grow in popularity, as Sister Catherine took charge of the Workroom in 1905. Lady Dudley ordered two dozen elaborate nighties as a gift to Margaret, daughter of the Duke of Connaught, who was to marry Prince Gustavus Adolphus of Norway and Sweden.

There were nuns constantly visiting from abroad in search of postulants for convents in

England, America and Australia. Three girls from the Industrial School left Cobh on September 8th on the "Campania" of the Cunard line, bound for Arkansas. There was an accident in which five people were killed and twenty-one injured. It was the first accident of a Cunard line ship in sixty years. We can only imagine the anxiety in St.Joseph's Convent until news was received that their girls had arrived safely at their destination.

By the year 1906 Irish had been introduced into the schools. Nineteen pupils from the convent schools were presented for inspection and all did very well in their native tongue.

News of an awful earthquake in San Francisco, California caused great concern in Kinsale. The whole city was damaged, as the fires resulting from the earthquake raged throughout the city, thankfully the Sisters were safe.

Another great loss was experienced by the community in 1907 with the death of Fr.Ronan S.J. who had been chaplain to the British forces in the Crimea and had a life long association with Kinsale. He had been a friend of Mother Francis.

Many letters 'toed and froed' between Lady Aberdeen and the children of the Industrial School whom the lady had taken to her heart.

In 1909 the telephone communication system was set up between the schools.

People from other Convents were constantly coming to Kinsale to view the Industrial School, and to seek advice on the setting up of a similar institution in their home Convents. The Authorities always regarded Kinsale as a model for other Industrial Schools.

1910 saw the death of Edward the Seventh. The children had a day off school for the funeral. Sr.Catherine gave the girls from the Workroom a day out in Cork. One hundred and forty three of them went by special train. Each one was given one and sixpence for refreshments and spending money. The archives record "They had a great day".

Two girls from the Industrial School, Dolly Hix and Mary Scully, left to go as postulants to South Africa.

The lodge, Marymount - later to become the staffroom for the staff of Our Lady of the Rosary School - was built for the convent gardener in 1913.

In the same year the subject of the Sisters' training as primary teachers arose. This programme began in the schools and was to last for three years at one hour per day. It was decided to set up a Training School in each convent, which had a National School. This was to happen by January 1914. A capable person, possibly a University Graduate, was to be appointed as superintendent and exams would be taken annually.

The lace industry proved to be a great advantage to the town, giving employment to the women and girls, as the men prepared for the "War, which was to end all wars."

Many soldiers were received into the Catholic Church during the year.

War broke out in August 1914. This had a profound effect on the town, as fathers, husbands, sons and brothers were called up - often as many as two or three from each family. As there was a great demand for horses, the Sisters lost their trusted "steed."

Sister Alacoque, known as "The Converts' Nun," because she instructed and prepared the soldiers for reception into the Catholic Church and for the reception of the Sacraments, received a letter from one of her "converts" Dr.Holdway of the First East Surrey Regiment, asking for prayers for them, as they were the first group going to "the front." Corporal A.Stepto of the 17th Infantry Brigade wrote giving news of his whereabouts. He was in Cambridge awaiting transfer to Belgium, and he asked her to visit his wife. Sister received several letters from her "boys", bearing news of injury and worse. She delivered messages to wives, mothers, sweethearts, etc. and kept the soldiers and their families constantly in the prayers of the community.

The town was experiencing great hardship during the war. As most of the men were away fighting and the businesses were in depression, people were susceptible to illness. By December there was an outbreak of scarlatina and whooping cough in the town, causing further deaths and hardship. Within the Church, Benedict XV was elected Pope in September.

In 1915 five Sisters, in compliance with orders from the bishop, prepared to take the King's scholarship a teaching qualification. Kitty Leahy who was the senior monitress came first in Ireland in her exams.

The 1916 Rising was not mentioned by the Convent Archivist: possibly news did not reach Kinsale until it was all over. They had a day of Prayer to end the war, and had begun baking their own bread. In September of that year, Dr.Coholan became Bishop of Cork.

1918 brought the anxiety of conscription. The Sisters were praying that this would not happen, and of course it didn't. There was a great interest in Irish Culture and language awakening in the people. The children from the convent took part in a local Feis and were well praised for their singing in their native tongue. In July Sister Catherine Blake celebrated her Golden Jubilee. Her workers put on a concert for her - there was much singing and dancing, including a poem, which they had written as a tribute to their "Boss".

In November the schools had to close due to a serious outbreak of influenza which came to be called "The Plague".

November 11th was a day of celebration to mark the end of the war.

By December the 'flu epidemic was on the wane, but the hospitals were still full. In March 1919 it raised its ugly head again. In November that year the Industrial School celebrated its Golden Jubilee with a huge party and concert.

The rise of Nationalism was becoming much more explicit in the 1920's. The children were taking part in feiseanna, Irish dancing and singing competitions. The Gaeltacht areas also seemed to be opening up - there is a record of Rita Murphy, one of the pupils, winning a scholarship to Ballingeary. It was recorded in the Annals that all schools were closed in protest against the treatment of Irish prisoners in Mountjoy prison. In September 1920 electricity was installed in the Convent. This work only took three weeks to complete, and the sisters were thrilled with the illuminations.

Sister Raphael O'Sullivan, whom many remember as an Infant teacher and a lady with an extraordinary sense of fun, contracted typhoid fever while at the General Novitiate at Belleville. Novices from St.Maries of the Isle, Bantry, Passage West and Kinsale made their novitiate together there. The other Kinsale novices at Belleville were Sr. M. Lawrence O'Neill, Sr.M.Evangelist O'Brien and Mother Enda Costelloe. It was not such a satisfactory arrangement so it closed in 1922 and was sold by public auction, realising the sum of £2000.

Mass was celebrated for the repose of the souls of Cork's Lord Mayor Terence McSwiney who died whilst on hunger strike in Brixton prison, and of Michael Fitzgerald who also died on hunger strike at Cork jail. A general day of mourning was declared and the schools were again closed.

The whole nation was thrown into mourning at the news of the shooting dead of Canon Magner by the Black and Tans. He being Sr.M.Alacoque's (the converts' nun) uncle, the news caused great distress in the convent.

1920 also saw the beginning of the decline of the lace making industry. Many of the senior workers married and some went to England with their soldier husbands. With cheaper, machine made products coming on the market the demand for the handcrafts was not so great.

Things seemed much calmer in 1921 - the calm before the storm. Sr.M.Raphael thankfully recovered from typhoid fever and was able to make her first profession. The health of Sr.M. Virgilius Fingleton - who later worked on the farm and in the gardens- continued to deteriorate. She had made her first profession on her sick bed and now her knee and finger problems continued. She was such a gentle and serene soul and despite very poor health lived into old age. She died in 1970, seven years after the celebration of her Golden Jubilee. The Peace Treaty was signed in December 1921. The annals record that twelve soldiers were received into the Church. It was also the year which saw the death of Sr.M.Catherine who had worked so hard with her girls in the lace workroom.

In January 1922 the Black and Tans and the R.I.C. left the town in lorries, and the barracks was taken over by the Irish Republican Party who hoisted the tricolour over the building. So many atrocities had been committed during the Black and Tan war that their departure was a great relief to everybody.

A more joyful event at the convent was a visit from Sr.Benignus Buckley, a former Industrial School child who returned from Arkansas, where she had gone to join a Religious Community eighteen years previously. No doubt she was amazed by all the changes which had taken place at her Alma Mater, and was delighted to see the Industrial School children taking part in the Feis and doing so very well.

The Irish Inspector visited the school and was delighted with the standard of Irish in all the convent schools. He reported that "the nuns deserve the highest praise for the excellent work they have done for the Irish Language."

Babs Collins

Mrs.Babs Collins whose family have lived for generations in Kinsale remembers happy days at the Convent schools.

"When I was going to school in the Convent, even though I didn't like school! The kindness that I experienced made it very enjoyable indeed. I remember my dear mother bringing me up my lunch each day and passing it in through the hatch in the door at the gable end (opposite MaryMount)

I remember Sister Mary Brendan who taught me when I was in either third or fourth class, because of her outstanding kindness and gentleness. She left a great impression on me. I also remember Sister Mary Kevin who taught music, also Sister Cecilia, Mother Enda, Mother Teresa, Mother Imelda and Mother Oliver.

The nuns took the children from the Industrial school on occasional outings to many places in the country. They primarily provided an education for many Kinsale people, who later on in life contributed a great deal to society. The nuns provided employment for many Kinsale people in the workroom. My mother remembered Mother Evangelist Fallon and Mother Catherine Blake.

When I was young I remember the Sisters visiting the sick, dying and housebound. They showed outstanding compassion to all in the community and made regular visits. I heard so much about their kind deeds and witnessed them myself I would like to wish them many happy years in their new convent.

In my opinion, what is needed in Kinsale at the present time is a closer community spirit, as there are many newcomers to the town. Also what is needed is a suitable venue where young people can meet and socialise in a pleasant environment. I also feel that greater community involvement in Church and Community related activities is needed."

Sadly at National level, it was the year of the Civil War, which caused so much pain and distress throughout the land, and under whose shadow the Irish Nation has lived until recent times.

In August the Barracks, the coastguard station, the fort and the police barracks were burned. It was a frightening time for the Sisters and the wider town community. There was so much shooting and military activity in Kinsale that the Director of the Sisters retreat had difficulty travelling and eventually he arrived by sea!

Tom Searls was busy repainting all those wonderful scrolls, with biblical texts, which adorn the stairway and top corridor. He made a really good job of them.

Again there were soldiers in the town - the Free State Army arrived in August.

There were sad scenes in 1923 when the Sisters had orders to vacate the hospital and former workhouse. What was to happen to the patients? A kind lady called Miss Bolton gave up her town house in Friar St. as a temporary hospital and some of the patients were transferred there. Others were taken to hospitals in Cork.

Sr.M.Emmanuel Lynch went to the Mercy Hospital to train as a nurse in 1925. She was the first sister to do so. The same year St.Therese of Lisieux, known as the "Little Flower" was canonised. The Community celebrated with extra prayers and they had a procession in her honour. Her relics have visited Ireland this year (2001) and Kinsale was one of the towns playing host to these, due to the presence of the Carmelite Friars in the town.

Typing, shorthand and bookkeeping were added to the many subjects already being taught in the Kinsale Industrial School.

Mr.Acton, who was so generous, annually provided wagonettes and motor cars to take the children of the Industrial School for a picnic in Garrettstown, which was one of the highlights of their year.

There was a massive measles epidemic with complications in 1926. Many people developed pneumonia as a result. The schools were closed for six weeks. It was not a good time for the town.

The town was still in a bad way in 1928. The local Council asked the Sisters to supply lunch to fifty or sixty children from the convent and monastery schools.

Unfortunately there was an outbreak of diphtheria in October. This caused the schools to be closed for a further three weeks.

The Industrial school and the nuns' cells were illuminated in 1931 thanks to the "Shannon Scheme". The new Cottage Hospital opened in September. Sr.M.Emmanuel and Sr.M.Xavier moved patients with their goods and chattels from Friar St., and Sr.M.Antonia and Sr.M.Cecilia received them at the other end into the fully transformed old workhouse hospital.

On December 12th Mercy Sisters everywhere celebrated the Centenary of the foundation of their order.

1932 was the year of the Eucharistic Congress. A year of great National importance, John McCormack our famous tenor who had been made a Papal Count in 1928 returned from America to sing during Mass in the Phoenix Park. Many people invested in the newly developed "wireless" to listen to this event.

Oil fired Central Heating was installed in 1934. This no doubt made a huge difference to the quality of life of the Sisters.

The Refectory decorated for Jubilee Celebration

Michael Cronin and his family have been neighbours and close friends of the sisters since the 1930's. They have been always available to the sisters in times of need.

"My first memory of the Convent would be in the nineteen thirties when I was three or four years old. Let us not be more specific than that. My mother took me to visit the nuns, where she

had been at school. Really, I suppose it would have been to parade her only boy. We got a great reception, of course, and I remember being surrounded by nuns and being asked what I would like to be when I grew up. In the emotion of the moment I said that I was going to be a nun, which went down very well indeed.

I went to school there myself in due course and I remember being in the "Babies class". Sister Rose, in a white veil was in charge of us all. There are still a few old classmates left in town and we reminisce now and then about things like the cakes and lemonade we had in the convent on our First Communion Day. A huge treat fondly remembered.

We went to live in one of the houses exactly across the road from the convent in about 1935. The nuns were good friends and neighbours but contact could only be made with them in the Convent. Whenever they went walking or on visitation in the town they always travelled in pairs and never spoke with the public. I remember many times meeting them on the Stony Steps and they would pass in silence with downcast eyes, like two ghosts. That was the rule and they had to keep to it.

Another memory is hearing the arrival of the hackney car every morning at 6.50 with the nuns from the hospital for the seven O'clock mass. In the cold and darkness of the winter it seemed like the middle of the night.

Over the years we had many good friends in the convent and still do. Breda, our children and myself think of them with affection and gratitude for the kindness shown and the prayers said."

The world was sadly at war once more in September 1939. This war lasted until 1944. Ireland did not take part in this fight against Hitler but many Irish men joined the British Army and are still remembered for their bravery.

1944 the Centenary year of the Convent. The celebrations, which began on April 12th, came to a climax with High Mass on April 19th, which was the actual foundation day. The Bishop Rev.Dr. Coholan presided. Father Johnson, a curate, from the Parish Church sang the Mass. The Sisters' choir rendered the music, with Sr.M.de Pazzi on the organ. Numerous priests and brothers attended. I believe the sanctuary was full! The sermon was delivered by Rev. Dr. Carmel O'Shea, Provincial O'Carm., a past pupil of St.Joseph's school. The Mass was followed by a huge banquet for the clergy and visitors in the community room and a similar spread in the refectory for the Sisters. In spite of the war, the Sisters had managed to provide a sumptuous feast. They prepared all of the food themselves. Numerous gifts were received including a telegram from Pope Pius X11 wishing the community, the schools and the hospital every blessing. The people of the town presented a large statue of St.Joseph, which still stands in the Convent garden.

Once the toasts and speeches had ended the assembled guests, with the Sisters, went to the Immaculate Conception room where a stage had been erected, and the curtain arose to reveal a choir of senior girls in white dresses and gold coatees singing the opening chorus of a Jubilee song. This was followed by the operetta "Pearl the Fishermaiden" which was presented by the children at the top end of the primary school, under the tuition of the very talented Sr.M.de Pazzi, assisted by the class teachers. The younger children's presentation - "The old woman who lived in a shoe" in their native Irish - delighted all present with their dazzling costumes as they enacted all the nursery rhyme favourites - Tom Thumb, Miss Muffett, Mother Goose, etc. The Secondary School pupils performed a play "St.Philomena". Following this treat, everybody returned to the Community room where they partook of High Tea, followed by a most enjoyable impromptu concert. Finally the day ended, the guests left and the Sisters went to the choir to offer thanks to God for the blessings of the hundred years just closed and to pray that a like munificent Providence would watch over the opening centenary.

Sister M.Finbarr Morrissey joined the community on the feast of Our Lady of Mercy during the centenary year. She recalls:

"September 24th 1944 marked the day of my entrance into Convent of Mercy, Kinsale. That was the Centenary Year of the foundation of the Convent. Could I not count myself as a centenary gift to the community? Happy years, structured and grace-filled, rolled onwards to 1972. This was a milestone on my life's journey - a journey that took me all the way to our Mission house in Delray Beach, Florida. Many lonely years followed as I missed dear old Kinsale, and all it stood for. However, we know that every cloud has a silver lining, and for me there is a silver highlight in every year as I wing my way back to the Alma Mater. Kinsale inspires me as I write, to an acrostic - style reflection on what my convent home means to me:

K is for Kindness showered on me by all,

I is for Inspiration and grace of my call,

N is for Nuns with a deep love of Christ,

S is for Sanctity and charity unbiased,

A is for Always my home here below,

L is for Loyalty and friendship aglow.

E is for Eternal rest to those gone before us –

"Suaimhneas síoraí acu sna Flaitheas"

Chapter 2
Kinsale's Family Tree

The Mercy roots had penetrated deep into the fertile soil of Kinsale. Strengthened by the prayer, example and spirituality of their foundress Catherine McAuley. They were now ready to branch out and answer the call for Mercy from wherever it came. The story of the spread of Mercy throughout Ireland and America is certainly a daring adventure and the very stuff of legend.

The Superior in the case of each foundation had to take responsibility for the welfare of her Sisters. Long negotiations were engaged in with the local Bishop who had to undertake to care for the Sisters, to see that daily Mass was said in their convent and that sufficient funds were available to finance the venture. The Mercy mission is to the poor, the sick and the marginalised, those who have no means of paying for care.

The Sodalities mentioned in all the foundations were of great significance. The members of the Sodalities were given Religious Instruction and they explored, with the aid of the Sisters, how the moral teachings of the Church could be applied to everyday life. The aim was to promote the spiritual welfare of the individual and to produce better-informed and more actively religious laity. This, of course, benefited the Church, as the members of the Sodalities were able to help the Sisters and Priests in their apostolates.

Kinsale Family Tree

2nd	3rd	4th	5th	6th	7th
Kingstown (1835)	Tullamore	Co. Cork	Carlow	Cork	(Co. Dublin)
Dunlaoghlaire		Charleville			Booterstown

14 Convents founded during Catherine McAuley's lifetime. Kinsale founded from Limerick

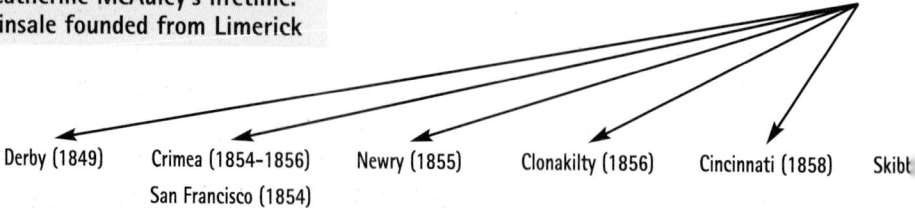

Derby (1849)	Crimea (1854-1856)	Newry (1855)	Clonakilty (1856)	Cincinnati (1858)	Skibt
	San Francisco (1854)				

Belper (1857-1860)	Sacramento (1857)	Rostrevor (1865)	Kilmacthomas Co. Waterford (1875-1878)	Chillocothe (1872)	Rossc
Carlton (1882-1889)	St Mary's Hospital (1857)	Lurgan (1866)	Waterford Workhouse (1876)	St. Patrick's Convent (1878)	Bodr
Atherstone (1893-1901)	Our Lady of Lourdes Oakland (1877)	Warrenpoint (1888)	Dunmore East (1883)	Urbana, Ohio (1878)	Boca
Mount Carmel St. (1899-1923)	(1854-1904) 5 convents San Francisco-Oakland area	Bessbrook (1889)	Jacksonville Florida (1960)	Bellefonteine, Logan County (1881)	
Highfields (1947)		Mobile, Alabama (1960)		London, Ohio (1883)	
Alvaston (1952)	By 1924 there were 28 institutions in California & Arizona			Piqua (1888)	
Swadlincote (1955-1991)	(1965) Acora, Peru			Delaware (1890)	
Beechwood (1968)				Hamilton (1891)	
				Linwood (1905)	

Mercy

blin

10th (London) Bermondsey	13th Birr	12th Wexford	11th Galway	9th Naas	14th Birmingham

**Kinsale made 9 foundations &
Workhouses (Youghal & Midleton)
& Crimea**

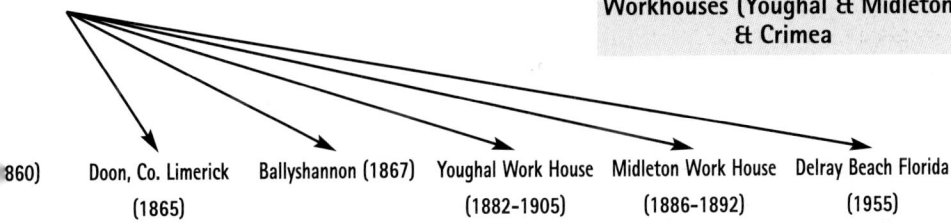

860)	Doon, Co. Limerick (1865)	Ballyshannon (1867)	Youghal Work House (1882-1905)	Midleton Work House (1886-1892)	Delray Beach Florida (1955)
894) wall orida	Thurles Cappamore Newport Fairoak, California	1891 Shiel Hospital 1898 St Patrick Workhouse Glenties 1899 St Joseph's Workhouse Stranolar 1900 Primary School, Glenties Workhouse, Donegal 1905 Primary School, Donegal 1919 Carrickboy Primary School 1958 "Stella Maris" Dungloe 1961 Sacred Heart Secondary School 1962 "Sancta Maria" Rosnowlagh 1964 Our Lady's Boarding School Ballyshannon 1966 Billings, Montana 1968 Secondary School Stranolar 1974 General Hospital Letterkenny 1977 St. Lukes Parish Great Falls			Port Charlotte (1967-1976)

Derby, Derbyshire, England
Convent of Mercy 1849

By 1849 the Community in Kinsale had grown sufficiently to be able to respond positively to a request for a foundation in Derby. Bishop Ullathorne and the Parish Priest, Father Thomas Sing, wrote to Mother Francis Bridgeman asking if she would send Sisters to minister in Derby.

Derby, very different from beautiful Kinsale, was situated in the heart of the British Midlands, miles from the coast. It was an industrial city, having silk, cotton and calico mills, a thriving porcelain trade – "Crown Derby" is still produced today.

It was an expanding city. Between 1800 and 1855 the population of Derby increased by 20,000, and between 1849 and 1860 over 300 Irish families, fleeing the Irish famine, made their way here.

Many of these famine refugees settled in some of Derby's worst slums, which were without drainage, had no laid on water or toilets and were often surrounded by large cess pools formed from the refuse of slaughter houses, tanyards, chemical works and drains. Their only water supply was from outside taps – one to every five families.

Other houses for the working class were small ill-ventilated and ill-lit cottages with mud floors. The social conditions were appalling. This would be the Sisters' first encounter with urban poverty.

The Holy Child of Jesus Sisters had vacated a Convent which would be given to the Sisters of Mercy. After all the negotiations were satisfactorily carried out the following Sisters were chosen for the mission: Sr Evangelist Benson, who would be Superior, Sr.Gertrude O'Dwyer, Sr. Agnes and Brigid Murrin. These Sisters left Kinsale on October 15th 1849, accompanied by Mother Francis and Sr.Joseph Lynch.

They arrived in Derby on October 17th and took up residence in the convent on Nottingham Road. The Bishop Dr.Ullathorne, and Fathers Sing and Daniel welcomed them and made sure they had all they needed to make themselves comfortable.

The Honourable Mrs.Beaumont, daughter of the Earl of Scarsdale, (Kedleston Hall, Derby), gave £3,000 as an endowment to the Sisters. This marked the first of many gifts from this generous lady. Miss Sing, sister of Fr.Thomas Sing, another generous lady, proved to be a great help to the Sisters in the foundation of the Convent.

The Catholic people of Derby were very poor, often destitute, and they worked mainly in the health destroying factories.

Mother Francis Bridgeman stayed six months to help establish the new foundation. This extended stay – a month was the customary stay of a Superior at a new foundation – was because of Mother Evangelist's poor health. Sister Joseph Lynch went home to Kinsale, and Sr. Camillus Delohoyd and Sr. Augustine Hickey came to assist the struggling community.

The early years were fraught with difficulty because of the acute bigotry and suspicion of the vast majority of Protestants. The Sisters were accused of proselytising and were often stoned or spat at in the streets. They were obliged to wear secular dress when they went on visitation. The visitation of the sick and poor was mainly to the Irish emigrants who had fled the Irish famine hoping for a better life!

When people saw what the Sisters were about; - caring for the children (many of whom they had to wash, feed and clothe before school began), and establishing an orphanage and House of Mercy, their fears were allayed and gradually a bond of love grew between the Sisters and people from all walks of life in the city, many of these people were of great financial and practical help to the work of the Sisters.

The community got their first postulant, Ann Leonard, in 1850. Her reception of the habit was the first public ceremony in the beautiful Convent Chapel at Nottingham Road.

The Convent was damp and unhealthy and this was affecting the health of some of the Sisters. Mrs. Scarsdale Beaumont came to their rescue by donating her own home 11 – 15 Bridge Gate, to become the new Convent for the Sisters of Mercy. She kept only a few rooms for her own use. When she left Derby in 1866 the Sisters turned her beautiful drawing room into a Chapel.

The Sisters carried on the work of the Mercy Order in and around Derby, visiting the poor and sick in their hovels and caring for the orphans and destitute young women as well as setting up many schools.

By 1857 Mother Evangelist took steps to spread Mercy around the British Midlands by opening a branch house in Belper, a country town about seven miles away. Sadly this had to close in 1860, as it became too expensive to run. A foundation in Carlton in 1882 closed seven years later for the same reason. The Atherstone foundation, which opened in 1893, closed in 1901 as many of the Sisters died of ill health. Subsequent foundations fared better, and I am happy to say that the Mercy Order is hale and hearty in the British Midlands thanks to the pioneering spirit of those early missionaries from Kinsale.

Strong links were retained between the Derby and the Kinsale communities. Mother Francis visited Derby again with the Sisters en-route to San Francisco in 1854. Imagine Mother Evangelist's delight tempered with sadness when she saw her sister, Sister Francis Benson, who was going so far away. On her way home from the Crimea Mother Francis stopped at Derby, and she visited the community again in February 1863. She retained a special affection for the first foundation she had sanctioned as Superior.

Sister Augustine Hickey and Sister Bernard Pearse spent three months in Kinsale in 1863 gaining some insight as to how the schools there were run.

Father Thomas Sing presented two identical statues of Our Lady, one to Kinsale and one to Derby. The Kinsale Annals record:

"On third of August 1854 a Munich Statue of the Blessed Virgin, the gift of Rev. Thomas Sing of Derby, arrived from England. It was brought in solemn procession to the altar prepared for it in the chapel, the Sisters wearing Church cloaks and bearing lighted tapers." This statue is still in the Chapel in Kinsale and the Derby statue is in a place of prominence within the Convent at Bridge Gate.

In 1893 Sister Evangelist O'Mahony became very ill, and it was decided that she might benefit from a visit to Kinsale. She set off accompanied by Sr. Baptist Everard. Sadly her health deteriorated and she died in Dublin. Her body then was taken to Kinsale for burial. Her grave can be seen in the old cemetery in the Convent grounds.

The "Munich Statue"

San Francisco
Convent of Divine Providence 1854

California was just four years a state, and in the throes of the gold rush. The Archdiocese of San Francisco was in the first year of its existence and in the charge of the thirty-six year old Dominican Archbishop. This young and dynamic Archbishop, Joseph Sadoc Alemany O.P., sent Father Hugh Gallagher to Europe to find desperately needed labourers for the Californian vineyard. The Archbishop specified the Sisters of Mercy as the congregation whose help he needed to meet the acute social needs of San Francisco – City of St.Francis - and Sacramento. Fr. Gallagher arrived in Baggot St. in July 1854 and talked with Mother Vincent Whitty, Mother McAuley's successor, at the Motherhouse. Mother Vincent directed him to Kinsale, which had been founded eight years previously and where there was a flourishing community. Having got permission from the Bishop of Cork, Dr.Delaney, Father Gallagher presented himself to Mother Francis Bridgeman. Mother Francis, having got the necessary written assurances that the spirit and rules of the congregation would be respected, asked for volunteers. She pointed out the difficulties of so distant a mission and the loneliness that the Sisters would experience in this rugged pioneer settlement. After a novena of prayer for the mission twenty-nine Sisters volunteered - almost the entire community! Bishop Delaney would only allow five professed Sisters to go on this foundation. Mother Francis chose very carefully those who would bring the Mercy flame to the New World. She selected five professed sisters and three novices. These included her aunt Sister M DeSales Reddan, who was fifty-four years old: Sister Mary Francis Benson who was thirty-eight years old and not in very good health (she spent forty-one years in San Francisco): Sister Mary Bernard O'Dwyer, noted for her piety and intelligence, was twenty-six years old and a noviceship companion of Mother Baptist: Sister Mary Howley, a twenty nine-year-old novice who outlived all the other Sisters living until 1907: Sister Mary Gabriel Brown aged twenty-five, and the youngest member of the group was Sister Mary Paul Beechinor. Sister Martha McCarthy, also aged twenty-six, proved to be an excellent teacher of small boys. Sister Baptist Russell, aged twenty-five, was appointed Superior of the group.

After six weeks' preparation the little group set off, accompanied by Mother Francis and Sr. Aquin Russell, Mother Baptist's sister, for Dublin. There they met their fellow travellers to the Californian mission – five Presentation Sisters heading for Sacramento, two Priests and two seminarians and, of course, Fr Gallagher –eighteen in all. Their passage had been booked on the "Arctic" for September 13th but because their number had grown since the booking the ship could not accommodate all of them so they decided to wait until they could all travel together. This was providential as the "Arctic" collided with another ship, went on fire and all on board perished. The little group secured a passage from Liverpool for September 23rd on the "Canada". This meant the Mercy group was able to visit their foundation in Derby. The Sisters in Derby were delighted to have the travellers with them and they were especially delighted to see Mother Francis again. Mother Evangelist Benson was no doubt delighted to see her sister, Sr. Francis Benson, but I suspect this joy was tinged with sadness, knowing that they would never meet again. On September 23rd they said good-bye to Mother Francis, Sr Aquin and the Derby sisters and set sail for the New World. Sr. Baptist used the thirteen-day trip to teach herself Spanish. When they reached New York they stayed at the Convent of Mercy, Houston Street, where they received a warm welcome, while their guide, Fr.Gallagher, attended to some business. The other members of the party went on ahead to California and arrived there three weeks before the Sisters of Mercy. The Kinsale contingent eventually set off in the company of a group of Jesuits, and five Notre Dame nuns, on the coastal steamer "Star of the West" which belonged to the Nicaragua Steamship Company. They travelled down the East Coast of America to the isthmus of Nicaragua in the company of miners who headed for San Francisco where they hoped to make their fortune from mining gold. It was a difficult journey as the ship was geared for the transport of prospectors and was rather rough and ready, not at all suitable for gentle young nuns.

When they reached San Juan del Norte, Nicaragua, all passengers and luggage were transferred into riverboats where they were packed like sardines. The heat was intense and it took several hours to reach the Castilian Rapids where they had to change again- this time onto a Steamer to cross Lake Nicaragua. The lake is very beautiful, 90 miles by 40 miles and is studded with islands, which are volcanic in origin. Two or three of these were active volcanoes. The full moon added to the beauty of this spectacular scene and the nuns were delighted with this awesome spectacle which proved to be the only pleasant part of a very arduous journey. There was a further transfer of passengers and luggage. This time the weary Sisters expected to travel the twelve miles through steep mountains on mules. To their delight large double seated wagons, each drawn by six mules, awaited them! Father Gallagher had somehow managed to secure this "luxurious" means of transport for them! They reached San Juan del Sur at about two o'clock in the morning. They had their first glimpse of the Pacific Ocean. They gazed in wonder at the magnificence of this wonderful ocean on whose shores they were to spend the remainder of their lives. As there were no piers they wondered how they would get to the "Cortez", the ship which was to take them on the final lap of their long journey, They saw men half-naked carrying ladies and gentlemen into the sea to the small boats which would take them out to their steamer anchored in the deep water. Presently the nuns' escort arrived, dressed in linen shirts and pantaloons – which Fr Gallagher had persuaded them to wear - and carried each Sister "my lady to London" style out to the skiffs. They reached the "Cortez" in time for supper which was a chaotic affair. Captain Cropper showed the Sisters great respect and tried to protect them from the motley array of wild people going west in search of gold. It took the "Cortez" thirteen days to make its way up the West Coast to San Francisco. Finally at midnight on December 7th they sailed into San Francisco Bay, ending a journey of 8,000 miles and three months of travel.

At five o'clock in the morning of December 8th 1854 Mother Baptist and her seven companions left the "Cortez" and landed in San Francisco. They made their way through the mud and dirt to St.Patrick's Church, arriving just as the priest was giving the final blessing. It was the day that Pope Pius 1X promulgated the dogma of the Immaculate Conception.

No home had been prepared for them and there was nobody to meet them. They went to stay with the Sisters of Charity who lived next door to the Church and who were caring for strays and orphans in an already overcrowded house. That afternoon Archbishop Alemany and the Vicar General came to welcome them.

For the next month the Sisters were glad to accept the kind hospitality of the Sisters of Charity, while they looked around for their new home and sought headquarters from which to begin their apostolate. In January they moved to a small house, consisting of six rooms and a kitchen, in Vallejo St. near the town's only hospital – The State Marine Hospital. They called it "The Convent of Divine Providence."

San Francisco had suddenly grown from a poor little hamlet in 1847 to a lawless city with little or no infrastructure when the Sisters arrived in December 1854. People were arriving there in their thousands because of the Gold Rush; the population had grown to 40,000 by the time the Sisters arrived. There were street fights and murders, and with men outnumbering women twelve to one it was not a safe place for women. Between 1849 and 1856 there were 1,000 murders and the courts were inadequate for the administration of justice. The prisons were full. The following extract from the City Annals gives some idea of the conditions the Sisters found in their adopted city:

"No praise can be given for the very dirty state in which the greater part of the town was allowed to remain... The streets were thickly covered with black, rotten mud. Rats, huge, fat, lazy things prowled around at pleasure. The pedestrian at night stumbling along the uneven pavements and through streets that were only a series of quagmires, would occasionally tread on one of the loathsome creatures and start back in disgust...at such a villainously unclean town.

Owing to the raising of the streets in the lower part of the city when establishing the bay, many of the building blocks became great hollow spaces surrounded on four sides by banks of earth.

Into these places which had no drainage every foul thing and unsightly rubbish were carelessly thrown, deep pools of stagnant waters collected there. Beneath the houses and streets which had been formed over the bay and which had been only partially filled up, there accumulated a vast mass of putrid substances from whence proceeded the most unwholesome and offensive odours."

This state of affairs clearly accounts for the high death rate in the city – between 1850 and 1854 there were 5,770 deaths!

In these early days there was much bigotry against Catholics and Irish people, generated by a secret society founded by New York bigots called the "National Council of the United States of North America" or the "Know Nothingists". This party grew rapidly and moved west with the Gold Rush. They were particularly active in American politics from 1852 to 1858. They viewed the arrival of the Sisters, who were both Irish and Catholic, with particular venom. They published articles against the Sisters making the most outrageous false accusations, saying: *"They did not keep the Sabbath and drank hard"* and many more equally scurrilous accusations. The Sisters made no attempt to refute any of the charges made against them, but when the Captain of the "Cortez," Captain Cropper, read these in the San Francisco Herald he was horrified. He wrote a letter to the "Herald" defending the Sisters and accusing the bigots of *"the most detestable calumny,"* saying: *"Their Religious exercises were performed, not only on Sundays but everyday, by themselves without intruding on others. In regard to 'hard drinking', I cannot imagine how any person could be so base a character as to slander them. The extreme propriety of their deportment, their unobtrusiveness, the gentle lady-like manners of the Sisters and the perfect correctness of the Fathers should have shielded them from so gross an outrage."* This seemed to quieten the bigots for a while.

The Sisters launched themselves into the works of Mercy in the city: the visitation of the sick and poor in their homes and with hospital work. They started the Sodalities and a night school for adults, as well as a Magdalen House for girls who were at risk in the city.

San Francisco, the chief port on the Pacific, observed no health regulations and so was wide open to Asiatic Cholera when it arrived in September 1855. The whole city was thrown into chaos, as the Civil Authorities had no idea how to deal with this crisis.

Mother Baptist and the Sisters who had experienced the 1849 cholera outbreak in Kinsale offered their nursing services. During the next six weeks they provided 'round the clock' care for the victims and helped to restore calm to a frightened city. The following extract from "The San Francisco Daily Times" of September 16th 1855 shows a vast change in public opinion regarding the Irish nuns:

"We visited yesterday the patients in the State Marine Hospital; a more horrible and ghastly

sight we have seldom witnessed. In the midst of the scene of sorrow, pain, anguish and danger were some four or five nuns who disregarded everything to render aid to their distressed fellow creatures. The Sisters of Mercy (rightly named) whose Convent is opposite the hospital, as soon as they learned of the state of matters, hurried to offer their services. They did not stop to enquire whether the poor sufferers were Protestants or Catholics, Americans or foreigners, but applied themselves to their relief. One nun would be seen bathing the limbs of a sufferer, another chafing the extremities, another applying remedies for the disease, while still another, with a pitying face, was calming the face of the dying. The idea of danger never seemed to occur to these women in the performance of the vows of their Order; they heeded nothing of the kind. If any of the stricken are saved, they will in a great measure owe their lives to these ladies."

The City Authorities asked the Sisters to take over the care of the sick on a contract basis. Mother Baptist agreed on condition that the entire control and employment of staff be left to her, so the Sisters bought the hospital for $14,000 which they borrowed at interest. The board of supervisors then rented the building from them at $400 a month. In October 1855 they took charge of this hospital. Mother Baptist's first action was to dismiss the entire staff of nurses, consisting of rough brutal men; the notion of female nurses had not yet reached California. The Sisters then set about cleaning the place thoroughly and fitting out as wards three rooms, which had been used previously by the attaches of the hospital. One of the upstairs rooms they set aside as a chapel.

The board of supervisors did not meet their part of the contract, so in March 1857 Mother Baptist had to tell them that it was not possible for the community to carry the city's burden unaided. The board of Supervisors still refused to pay their share, so the Sisters had no choice, due to financial difficulties, but to stop accepting patients. At the young age of twenty-nine Mother Baptist learned a harsh lesson on the workings of the government of the city of San Francisco – the City of St.Francis!

July 27th 1857 saw the beginning of a new era in health care in San Francisco with the opening of St. Mary's Hospital in an old brick hotel on Stockton St. It marked the opening of the first Catholic hospital on the Pacific coast, staffed with the best doctors. It served as a working base for much of the medical progress in California. The humble Dominican Archbishop was often seen in his patched robes visiting the patients at this place of healing.

On July 22nd 1857 Mother Baptist Russell and Mother de Sales Reddan went by river steamer to Sacramento with a view to opening a branch house there. The journey, which now takes two hours by train or car, took a day and a night then. On Friday October 2nd of the same year Mother Baptist led a group of five Sisters to establish the first Convent of Mercy in

Sacramento, one hundred miles northeast of San Francisco. The following Monday, October 5th , they opened a school in the basement of the church and sixty-five children turned up. By the end of the term the number had doubled.

Malaria, scurvy, diarrhoea, dysentery typhoid fever and numerous other diseases were rampant in this city. The Sisters were kept busy during their after school hours and at weekends looking after the sick. In 1860 they built a new Convent dedicated to St.Joseph, and in 1886 Sacramento became an independent foundation. Until 1901 the Sisters of Mercy were the only Sisters in Sacramento.

A new hospital, which opened in November 1861, was built on a hill overlooking the bay in San Francisco. This second St. Mary's Hospital was built from money collected from miners, the proceeds of a Ladies' Fair and a benefit performance put on by the Players from the Metropolitan Theatre. Between them they raised over $15,000, and a Mr. P.H. McMahon left his entire estate of $650 to the Sisters, which they added to the fund.

The hospital opened its doors to twenty-seven patients and half the community from the "old hospital". For forty- five years this St. Mary's was a famous landmark of early San Francisco and from there Mercy, charity and benevolence radiated throughout the city.

During the financial depression of 1875 hundreds of men, young and old, were served food in a temporary pavilion which had been erected in the courtyard of St. Mary's. In 1893 the city found itself once more in the grip of another depression. Seven hundred distressed poor were served Christmas Dinner in the same courtyard.

Religious instruction classes were conducted in this famous building. In 1871 Our Lady of Mercy school opened and thirty-nine girls arrived on the first morning. By the end of the month the number had grown to one hundred and seventy- eight. 1872 saw the opening of a house for the aged and infirm of the city. An Industrial Training School was opened where girls were taught various skills to aid them in finding employment. There was an employment agency attached to the Industrial School. This found well over 1,000 jobs for poor applicants every year. Later the Mater Misericordia hostel opened. This was a residence hall for women and girls who were out of work.

Members of the women's sodality, which had grown to 1,000 since its foundation in 1859, were a great help to the Sisters in their apostolic work.

The Motherhouse and Novitiate, also housed on the hill, were kept busy with the constant flow of novices. There were annual receptions and professions.

When the City's Industrial School for juvenile delinquents had to close in 1869 due to mismanagement, Mother Baptist was asked by the investigating grand jury to take sixty-three girl inmates into Magdalen House.

In 1877 a branch house was opened across the bay at Oakland, which was then a far cry from the "Athens of the Pacific" as it is known today.

The Sisters came again to the aid of the stricken city during the smallpox epidemic of 1868, which spread the entire length of the Pacific coast, causing countless deaths. It has been estimated that one person in forty-eight died of the disease. Miraculously none of the Sisters caught this dreadful disease.

The Spanish American war broke out on April 21st 1898. San Francisco became a base for military operations. The military facilities were inadequate for the number of men so typhoid and pneumonia broke out in alarming epidemics. Four Sisters of Mercy were sent to nurse the soldiers.

Mercy in San Francisco had developed with the city, and Mother Baptist won the title of "Mother of the City", but sadly her time was coming to an end. She died on August 6th 1898. Mother Columba Kelly succeeded her as superior.

Today of course there are twenty-eight Mercy institutions in California and a Mission in Peru. From little acorns great oak trees grow.

I leave the last word on this foundation to Sister Mary Aurelia McArdle RSM California:

"Just eight years after her peaceful death within its walls, the "Hospital on the Hill" was destroyed in the flames that claimed the historic heart of San Francisco. And just as the "city loved around the world" rose again from its ashes, so also did a new and splendid St. Mary's again lift up the cross and scalpel to serve God and mankind in the tradition of its well loved Foundress, Mother Mary Baptist Russell." - California's Pioneer Sister of Mercy.

Catherine McAuley's friend Dr.Michael Blake, Bishop of Dromore, recommended that Catherine, known as Kate Russell, enter the Convent of Mercy Kinsale, provided she return and found a Convent in her home town of Newry, when the time was right. God however had other plans for Kate – Mother Baptist as she became – and she set off for San Francisco!

Subsequently Elizabeth Russell, Kate's sister, entered Kinsale on the provision that she and her dowry would return to Newry as soon as "Mercy" could be established there.

It seems that plans were already afoot for this foundation as the Kinsale Annals records:

"Before leaving for the East (Crimea) Mother Francis Bridgeman had entered into negotiations with most Rev.Dr.Blake, Bishop of Dromore and his Co-Adjutor most Rev.Dr.Leahy concerning a filiation in Newry. Their Lordships agreed to allow £100 per annum for the support of the Sisters, to appoint a chaplain to say Mass daily for them and to pay the rent of the Convent while necessary."

In 1855 the Coadjutor Bishop, Dr.John Pius Leahy O.P., and Father Patrick O'Neill, Administrator of Newry, collected funds for the Mercy foundation. A committee was formed and collections were carried out on a weekly basis. The people of Newry were extremely generous and contributed handsomely to these weekly collections. Margaret Russell, mother of the Russell sisters, contributed £700 to the project. They were soon able to buy Ogles Big House in Canal St. as a temporary Convent, as well as having money in the bank to support the Sisters.

The following Sisters were chosen for the Mission: Sister Catherine O'Connor (Superior), Sisters Agnes Burke and Elizabeth Martin (both of whom were subject to recall) and Sisters Aquin (Elizabeth) Russell and Bridget who were novices. Sr.Aquin was considered the Foundress of this Convent. On June 21st 1855, with Fr.Patrick O'Neill as guide, the little group left the Motherhouse in Kinsale. Having rested at St.Catherine's Baggot St. Dublin, they continued to Newry, arriving on June 26th. They were welcomed warmly by the clergy and some ladies from the town. They immediately set to work establishing Mercy. Visitation of the sick began in July 1855. The first inmate of the House of Mercy was a little deaf and dumb girl. They opened a public laundry to train girls and give them a means of support.

the town was the domain of the Poor Clare Sisters who ran the schools. Dr.Blake ve permission to the Sisters of Mercy to open schools, except for girls over twelve years of age. They established an Industrial School, called - a Sewing School - to differentiate from the Government Industrial School. Here the girls could earn their livelihood by needlework. They produced beautiful work here, plain and fancywork as well as the famous Limerick Lace. The girls' work was sold as far afield as Australia and New Zealand and it won prizes and awards at the various exhibitions in Ireland and England.

The first postulant, Elizabeth Callen from Dundalk, arrived in February 1856. Significantly, Sister Aquin was the first novice to make her profession as a Sister of Mercy in Newry on March 26th 1856. Drs.Blake and Leahy officiated and a large crowd attended.

In 1958 the Honourable Mrs.Ross of Bladenburg asked if the Sisters would take over the orphanage under her patronage at Rostrevor. The Sisters were delighted to oblige. Twelve children were brought to Canal St. and so began the Mercy Orphanage in Newry.

The House of Mercy and Orphanage were merely outhouses, set up for those purposes.

Hannah Moylon had been brought from Kinsale to teach lace and goldwork. Imagine the great joy when she entered the Newry Community.

St. Joseph's Society was established in December 1859 for the women who had been attending Sunday school.

Soon the "temporary" convent was too small for the rapidly growing community. A site was found and a new Convent was built. Mr.Burke who designed the Mater in Dublin was the architect of a four-storey building with a frontage of one hundred and one feet and which was fifty feet in depth. The Convent opened in 1862. Mrs.Russell again showed her generosity by donating the altar.

January 1862 also saw the founding of The Ladies' Clothing Society for work among the poor.

Amid great excitement in 1863 a postulant, Isabella Vanderstraaten, entered from far away Ceylon (Sri Lanka as it is now known).

The Sodality of the Children of Mary was founded in 1864.

By June 1865 a branch house was established at Rostrevor. Mother Aquin Russell was to take charge of this foundation accompanied by Sr.Teresa, Sr.Evangelist and Sr.Zita.

1865 was a busy year for the growing community: A night school for the girls who worked in the mills was started and the Sisters were asked to open a Convent in Lurgan.

No suitable building could be found in Lurgan so land was purchased and a Convent and a school were built. On August 20th 1866 Sr.Emmanuel Russell (the third of the Russell sisters), Sr.Francis, Sr.Angela, Sr.Vincent, Sr.Magdalen and Sr. Stanislaus were the founding Sisters there, Sr.Emmanuel being Superior.

The Convent Secondary School, Newry, started as a room in the Convent. The Community bought a house adjoining the Convent in Canal St.where they opened a School for Infant boys.

A benefactor, Mr. Thomas Fagan bought a house and garden in Kilmorey St. and gave it to the Sisters to be run as "A Home for Respectable, Destitute Females of the Town."

November 1887 saw the opening of an Intermediate School on the ground floor of the Convent in Canal St. That same year a branch house opened at Warrenpoint.

The Bessbrook foundation was made on May 4th 1895.

The Convent Chapel, known as "Emmanuel Chapel", was built as a result of a donation of £2,000 made by the widow of Lord Charles Russell of Killowen (brother to the Russell sisters). Lady Russell gave a further £1,000 as a gift to her sister-in-law, Mother Emmanuel. This was added to the previous donation. Unfortunately Mother Emmanuel, who died on March 8th 1902, never saw this Chapel named in her honour which opened on July 20th 1904. Her surviving brother, Father Matthew Russell, preached at the opening.

This Foundation has grown and developed over the years. Since 1960 the Newry Sisters have had a foundation in Mobile, Alabama. Contact has been maintained with the Motherhouse. Sr.Aquin Mulvey, who trained as a nurse and suffered for many years from the effects of T.B., came to Kinsale as a postulant from Newry. She was a very talented artist, spending much of her time painting and knitting.

Clonakilty, Co. Cork
Convent of the Sacred Heart 1856

On the feast of St.Catherine of Siena, April 30th 1856, at the request of Fr. Morgan Madden P.P. four Sisters left for Clonakilty to staff the school which he had built for the education of Catholic children.

Rev.Mother Teresa Maher, Sr.Genevieve O'Donoghue who was to be the Superior, Sr.Philomena Maher, Sr.Camillus DelaHoyde and Sr.Magdalen Lordan left Kinsale accompanied by Fr.Madden and the Parish Priest of Kinsale, Fr.Kelleher. They were given a furnished cottage as a Convent, which at first was intended as a branch house, but later became a foundation.

The school which had been built on extensive grounds was impressive – three storeys high and in readiness for the education of Clonakilty's children.

The day following their arrival the Sisters were visited by the Bishop of Ross, Rev.Dr.Keane, and by priests from the surrounding parishes. The townspeople also came to welcome them – many came just to get their first sight of a "nun".

The Immaculate Conception Primary School opened on May 19th 1856. Fr.Madden walked the children – 800 of them - from the Parish Church to their new School and left them in the care of the Sisters. 800 children to four Sisters – what a task, but of course they were Sisters of Mercy and they managed 200 children each! They took the names of the children and classified them according to their knowledge. The subjects taught were Religious Instruction, the "Three R's", needlework, embroidery, printing and singing. The Sisters both worked and managed the school, which was not recognised by the National Board until June 1857. Father Madden supplied the school with books and equipment.

On March 25th the orphanage opened - Elsy, a five year old little girl whose mother had died, was placed in the care of the Sisters. Soon there were twelve such little girls and so the orphanage developed. As with each new foundation visitation of the sick and poor in their homes began immediately, the Sisters trying to alleviate some of the poverty and hardship being experienced.

By 1861 the cottage was unfit for habitation so the Sisters moved into the top storey of the school. Four years after their arrival they undertook a huge building programme which lasted three years. This gave employment to the local tradesmen and labourers at a time of great distress and poverty. The Sisters received many donations which helped finance this major project. The Convent was completed in 1864 and called "Our Lady of Mercy of the Sacred Heart."

An Infant School for boys opened in October 1867, and St.Aloysius' Industrial School opened in 1869

The Community grew and grew and by 1875 the Sisters were able to start a foundation of their own in Kilmacthomas, Co.Waterford. Unfortunately closed in 1878. The Sisters took up duty at the Waterford City Workhouse in 1876.

In 1887 the Sisters took charge of the hospital in Clonakilty. Sr.Bernadette Leahy came from Kinsale to help with this project. She stayed three years.

When the Sisters took over the Workhouse, people from all the Workhouses in West Cork were sent there. It became known as "The West Cork County Home."

The Sisters provided secondary education in 1908. The Sacred Heart Secondary School opened in 1941, and in 1956 a Boarding School was provided.

Four Sisters set off for Jacksonville, Florida, on August 25th1960.

In 1968 the then Bishop of Cork, Dr.Cornelius Lucey, visited Clonakilty and asked for a Sister to join the Cork Mission to Trujillo, Peru. Sr.Kevin O'Brien, who is now part of the Kinsale Community, responded to the call and joined the Bantry Sisters. She worked in Peru from 1968 to 1974.

Convent of Mercy, Clonakilty has associations with the Benedictine monk and Abbot of Maredsous in Belgium, the Blessed Dom Columba Marmion. Three of his sisters joined the Clonakilty Community. Sr.Columba (Lizzy) entered on August 4th 1870. In 1876 she and two other Sisters from Clonakilty went to open a school in Kilmacthomas later in the same year she went to take up duty in John's Hill, Hospital Waterford City. In 1883 Sr.Columba Marmion founded the Convent of Mercy in Dunmore East, She died in 1918 and is buried in the cemetery of the Convent of Mercy, Waterford. Flora Marmion – Sr.Lorenzo came to the Convent in Clonakility on July 2nd 1873. She died there in 1892 when she was thirty-nine years old. The third Marmion sister – Rosie (Sr.Peter) entered Clonakilty Convent and spent her life there, she was Novice Mistress for several years and served three terms as Superior. She died in 1930. Blessed Marmion kept up regular correspondence with his sisters and visited Clonakilty several times, where he gave conferences to the Sisters and celebrated Mass in the Convent Chapel.

Two Kinsale past pupils who entered the Convent of Mercy Clonakility were Sr.Benedicta Barry and Sr.Eugenius O'Donovan.

Cincinnati
Convent of the Divine Will 1858

For many years Archbishop Purcell of Cincinnati had been anxious to introduce the Sisters of Mercy into his diocese. He commissioned Mrs.Sarah Peter, a benevolent convert and daughter of the sixth Governor of Ohio, to make application on his behalf.

On May 3rd 1856 Mrs.Peter arrived at the door of the Convent of Mercy, Kinsale, too late for visiting, but she insisted on seeing the Superior, Rev.Mother Teresa Maher.

Thus began the negotiations for the Cincinnati foundation. When the Bishop of Cork, Dr. Delaney, and Rev.Mother Teresa Maher were satisfied that all the conditions for the protection of the Sisters would be met by Archbishop Purcell, they consented to the foundation. The following Sisters were chosen for this difficult mission: Five professed Sisters – Mother Teresa Maher, Sister Gertrude O'Dwyer, Sister Baptist Kane, Sister Stanislaus Murphy and Sister Francis Noonan. These Sisters were very young, Sister Stanislaus being eighteen and Sister Francis only seventeen. Four Novices; Sister Xavier Scully, Sister Joseph Leahy, Sister Ursula Kenny and Sister Mary Campbell; a postulant Agnes McCoy, and a young aspirant, Hannah Kiely, completed the group of eleven.

On July 23rd 1858 at six o'clock in the morning the group left Kinsale for Cork, from where they sailed to Bristol. They stayed a few days with the Sisters of Mercy in Bristol and travelled to Southampton by train on July 28th. They met Mrs. Peter in Southampton and went aboard the "Arago" which was to take them to New York. The voyage lasted thirteen days. It was not a pleasant crossing and the Sisters suffered from seasickness. In between bouts of seasickness they walked on the decks, gave assistance where it was needed, read and did some sewing. They kept apart as much as possible from the other passengers. They saw an iceberg, a school of porpoises and other boats, which helped to break the monotony of the journey. The scenery charmed them as they sailed into New York harbour. On the 9th August they landed in New York and were warmly welcomed by the Sisters of Mercy in Houston St. where they stayed until August 17th, when they set off for Cincinnati. The weather was intensely hot and oppressive, making this lap of the journey most unpleasant. The monotony of the journey was broken only by the glimpses they got as they passed cities like Philadelphia and Pittsburgh. Sight of the Allegheny Mountains, the Susquehanna River, the hills of Virginia and the Prairies delighted them. Dusty and fatigued after forty hours continuous travel they arrived in Cincinnati.

Cincinnati, Ohio's third largest city, is situated between the Great Miami and the Little Miami rivers and is surrounded by hills. An Industrial city with a large pork- packing centre, it emerged as a port after 1811 when the first Steamboat in Western waters arrived from Pittsburgh. In 1842 it was one of the few cities admired by Charles Dickens. In 1858 it had a population of 200,000 people, 50,000 of whom were Catholic. There was a lot of poverty and illiteracy in the city especially among the newly arrived Europeans. Many Irish, fleeing the poverty of home, had settled there. Prostitution was rife in the city among girls who had neither family nor means of livelihood, so there was much work for the Sisters to do in their new home.

Mrs. Peter's home at Lytle St. had been prepared for the Community as a temporary Convent until a suitable house could be found for them. The Archbishop came to welcome them the day following their arrival, August 19th 1858. He celebrated Mass and blessed their "Convent" naming it "The Convent of the Divine Will." August 24th, Feast of St. Bartholamew, was named Foundation day.

The Community began their mission with a retreat from September 5th to 14th. They stayed with Mrs. Peter until October 11th when they moved into their own Convent. This was a house in Sycamore St. behind St. Thomas' Church. It was in a frightful state of filth as well as being damp, airless and neglected. They had no furniture, only beds which had been given by a kind benefactor and their kitchen table was a plank of wood across two barrels! The poor of Cincinnati were kind and generous and soon they had supplied the Sisters with all the necessities of life. A collection was made at the local Churches to help pay for the repairs necessary to part of this house which was to become a House of Mercy.

They opened schools in the basement of the Church. A night school attended by almost two hundred girls opened on October 25th , and on October 26th an infant school for boys opened. Over eighty boys attended this school.

A huge crowd attended the reception ceremony of the postulant Sr.Agnes McCoy. The Archbishop preached, the Church Choir sang and the novice elect was adorned in Limerick lace, flowers and jewellery. It made a wonderful impression on all present.

The children from the night school, knowing Mother Teresa to be an accomplished pianist, gave the Sisters a piano for Christmas, which no doubt helped them to spend a joyful first Christmas away from their beloved St.Joseph's.

On February 2nd 1859 they received their first American postulant, Ellen Doherty, and Hannah Kiely who came out from Kinsale with the Sisters joined the community as a postulant.

As the Convent, which could not be kept warm in winter or cool in summer, was having an adverse effect on the health of the community, Mother Teresa asked the Archbishop for his permission to purchase a more suitable property. Permission granted, Mother Teresa went ahead and bought a German Orphanage, which extended from 3rd to 4th Street.

Large confraternities and sodalities were formed. The Sisters fed over one hundred unemployed people each day. They harboured thousands of destitute women regardless of colour, class or creed. Much found refuge at the Convent during the devastating floods.

A laundry was opened to give employment to young women.

According to an 1858 Newspaper account the Sisters' work in the City included : *"taking care of young children while mothers worked and providing a home for young girls who were out of work. They visited hospitals and jails, sick and destitute in every part of the city, bestowing kindness on all regardless of religion or nationality. They ran classes for married women, a Sunday school of two hundred youths and a Wednesday School for as many more. Religious Instruction was provided for over a thousand families. There was a laundry where destitute women were employed and paid the going rate for their work, and a sewing room which employed women to do the most exquisite needlework"*.

At their reception ceremony on September 24th 1859 Ellen Doherty took the name Sister Mary of Mercy, and Hannah Kiely was known as Sister Mary Angela.

Towards the end of this year, 1859, an accident occurred which caused hardship to several families. A church wall fell on thirteen men crushing them to death. Eleven of the men had young families. Collections were held in all churches in the city – Catholic and Protestant – to help the bereaved families

On June 4th 1860 the Community moved into their new Convent which was large enough to house schools, House of Mercy and Industrial School as well as any future works that the Sisters might undertake.

The early years were extremely difficult as many young Sisters died of consumption, resulting from the appalling conditions of their first Convent, the rigours of the American climate and long hours of strenuous work. In 1860 Sister Joseph Leahy who had come from Kinsale died, and in 1861 Sr.Xavier Scully, another of the pioneers, died. Even though they seemed to be getting many postulants, the number of deaths was very worrying, so Mother Teresa and Mother Baptist returned to Kinsale in November 1864 on a recruitment mission. They stayed over six months, returning in April, 1865, with six Sisters from their homeland – one professed Sister from Kinsale, Sr.Gertrude Dobbyns; a novice, Sr.Aloysius McCarthy from Skibbereen Convent of Mercy, and four postulants. They were shocked on their arrival to hear of the assassination of President Lincoln. They also returned to a crisis of vocations and donations caused by the Civil War. As a solution to the financial crisis Mother Baptist Kane, a scholar who read and spoke French, wrote a book for American Catholics called "The Help of Christians – A Manual of Instructions and Prayers compiled from Approved Sources". Archbishop Purcell was delighted with the publication of this badly needed book and worked hard to market it. Mother Teresa gave music lessons which no doubt further taxed her already overtaxed resources.

During the Civil War the Military rented part of their house for prisoners of war and sick and wounded soldiers. The Sisters helped nurse the sick. They continued to visit the prisoners until the last one was released in 1865.

In February 1862, the Mayor of Cincinnati asked the Archbishop for Sisters to nurse the Ohio regiments injured at the Pittsburgh Landing (a wharf from which cotton was shipped to Tennessee). Mother Teresa headed the group of Sisters selected for this "Mission". They went downriver to the scene of the slaughter which followed the fierce battle. There was a huge number of dead and wounded. Many good local ladies came to help, but when smallpox broke out they fled, and the Sisters were left to face that particular danger alone. They worked ceaselessly among the victims of this horrible disease until the patients were eventually removed to the base hospitals.

Again in 1866, when cholera broke out in the city, the Mayor asked the Sisters to convert their house on Third St. into a hospital. Control of the hospital was given to the Sisters who worked day and night to alleviate the suffering of the plague victims.

In 1868 the Sisters decided to build a church. They bought a site beside the House of Mercy and began fundraising. Mother Baptist wrote and marketed a book called "A Guide for the Religious called Sisters of Mercy" as her contribution to the fund. The Sisters made every sacrifice possible to raise money. The Sodalities held a three-week Fair which raised $3,000. The Sisters held an exhibition of Munich Statuary, charging an entrance fee of a dime. Mother Baptist, in spite of all her pressing activities, got her pen out again and wrote another book- "Meditations According to the Method of St.Ignatius on the Sufferings, Life and Death of Our Lord Jesus Christ."

This Church was to cause much pain and heartache to the Sisters and was to implicate them in a scandal which was not of their making. A chaplain appointed to the Convent removed the Sodalities, which the Sisters had established over the years, in a most underhanded way to the Cathedral. This of course, caused outrage among the Catholic Community. Archbishop Purcell blamed the Sisters for causing this rebellion among the people. The Sisters had nothing to do with it, the people being able to make up their own minds. The Community first heard of the removal of the Sodalities from an announcement made at all the Masses in the city on the Sunday following the event. In 1873 the Archbishop asked the Sisters that the Church be deeded to him and that the House of Mercy be given to the "chaplain" as a pastoral residence for himself! Mother Teresa and the Sisters were aghast at this turn of events. They refused to give over the House of Mercy but had to part with the Church. They had already invested $60,000 in the land and the structure, causing great financial strain on the little Community. The Archbishop was to regret this ill treatment of the Sisters, as this Church became one of the casualties when the Purcell bank failed and the Diocese went bankrupt. Had it been in the hands of the Sisters it would have been saved the fate of the other Churches in the diocese, which had to be sold. Archbishop Purcell had to resign his Archbishopric, since it was his brother who ran the Purcell Bank.

Mother Teresa was on her death bed when this scandal broke and she dictated a letter to Mother Baptist, giving an account of the pecuniary affairs of the Convent from the first and declaring strongly that the Community was in no way connected with the financial difficulties under discussion.

Another distress was caused during the building of the Church in 1870 when excavations under the Convent were so deep that part of the Convent building had to be propped up by beams. The beams were inadequate and gave way under the pressure. The Sisters were terrified but kept up a constant vigil of prayer. In the moment of greatest danger a stone mason, Mr.McLoughlin, by his swift action and skill saved the Convent.

During the 1870's the Sisters went on recruiting missions around America. They were able to open a branch house at Cillicothe in August 1872. This was one of several branch houses to be established in various parts of the diocese between 1870 and 1880.

Their friend and benefactress, the lady responsible for bringing them to Cincinnati, Mrs. Sarah Peter, died in 1877. By this time also Mother Teresa's own health was in decline. She asked the Archbishop on several occasions to release her from her duties as Superior but he refused. I do not think anybody realised how ill she was, but she was aware that she suffered from a heart condition which claimed the lives of so many members of her family. She went on the doctor's advice, to a rented house in Kentucky, accompanied by two Sisters in June 1877.When she returned in September she seemed much improved, but sadly she died in November of that year, aged just 53 years. She had been Superior for eighteen of her thirty years as a professed Sister, three years in Kinsale and fifteen in Cincinnati.

Skibbereen, Co. Cork
Convent of the Immaculate Conception 1860

Skibbereen, a famine blackspot, welcomed the first Sisters of Mercy on May 24th 1860. Three professed Sisters: Sr.Philomena Maher (sister to Mother Teresa Maher who went to Cincinnati), Sr.Raphael Sexton, and Evangelist Fallon, as well as Sr. Martha Walshe, a novice, left St.Joseph's Kinsale. Sr. Philomena Maher was to be the Superior of this little group. The Convent and school were ready to receive them. The school opened its doors to five hundred pupils on June 4th. Visitation of the sick and poor began immediately.

Sr.Martha Walshe made her first profession on December 8th 1861 and took the name Sr.Mary Joseph.

By April 1868 the Chapel was completed and ready for use.

The Sisters wished to provide employment for young girls so that the flow of emigration could be stemmed. They started a weaving industry and contact was made with Sir William Ewart of Belfast. He gave the Sisters all the information they required as well as two new hand looms. Other generous benefactors followed his example and soon they had twenty-three looms. Some time later Sir William's son presented the Community with a Warping mill.

The weaving industry in Skibbereen and the surrounding areas survived until the outbreak of the First World War in 1914.

Between 1875 and 1879 the Sisters were admitted as nurses to the local Workhouse and in 1884 a Sister was appointed matron when the administration of the hospital was given over to the Sisters. Clinics on Cape Clear, 1879, and on Hare Island, 1886, were serviced from the Skibbereen Workhouse during outbreaks of typhoid and smallpox on these islands.

In 1894 a foundation was made in Rosscarbery, and in 1902 Sisters went to Bodmin in Cornwall to start a foundation there.

The new hospital in Skibbereen was built in 1925, providing accommodation for Sisters as well as patients. Today St.Anne's Hospital continues to care for the sick of the district.

In 1938 the Secondary School for girls was established, "Mercy Heights" being opened in 1971. Further ministry abroad occurred in 1971 when Sr.Alberta joined the Cork and Ross mission to Peru, labouring there for six years.

The Sisters from Skibbereen went to Boca Raton, Florida, in 1960 and opened a branch house there.

The new Primary School opened in 1982.

Skibbereen along with Kinsale and Clonakilty Sisters now form part of Mercy Ireland Southern Region.

Doon, Co. Limerick
Convent of the Divine Will 1865

Father Patrick Hickey, Parish Priest of Doon, Co.Limerick, bequeathed his property for the establishment of a Convent in Doon after his death. He was familiar with the Convent of Mercy, Kinsale, where his niece, Sister Augustine Hickey had already entered and was working in Derby. His great niece, the future Sister Patrick O'Brien was about to enter St. Joseph's, Kinsale. He requested that Sr.Patrick O'Brien would be one of the Sisters assigned to the Doon Convent and that any members of his family wishing to do so would be accepted into the Mercy Congregation.

Father Hickey died in 1864, and on September 12th of that year Rev.Mother Ligouri O'Dwyer of Kinsale and her Assistant, Mother Francis Bridgeman, visited Archbishop Leahy of Cashel to obtain his approval for the foundation. They also visited the site allocated to them in Doon and found it to their satisfaction. The Kinsale Annals record the Profession of Sister Patrick O'Brien on September 26th 1864 for the Doon mission. On February 1st 1865 Sr.Augustine Hickey was recalled from Derby, where she had laboured for fifteen years, to become Superior of the Doon Foundation. The remaining three members of the foundation were Sr.Teresa Fallon, Sr.de Pazzi Kilroe and Sr.Bridget Fitzgerald. These were later joined by Sr.Catherine Ryan who arrived with Sr.Augustine Hickey on February 27th. Rev.Mother Ligouri and Sr.Magdalen of Derby accompanied the group. They stayed overnight at the Charleville Convent of Mercy and continued to Limerick Junction by train the next day, from where they travelled by "Outside Cars" the remaining few miles to the village of Doon. Their luggage had to be left at the railway station since there was no room for it in the cars. It was picked up later by a kind villager.

They were welcomed by the Parish Priest and Curate and taken to their house – "a three up, two down" at the top of the street on the Cappawhite Road. Its front door opened out onto the street. This residence was musty and dusty and inhabited by spiders and mice when the Sisters arrived! The first evening they partook of their meal seated on the ground. On that evening also the Canon brought The Blessed Sacrament, so the house was now a convent. They named it "Our Lady of Mercy of the Divine Will."

The sleeping arrangements were rather cramped on that first night; the two Superiors slept on two sofas in the parlour while the five sisters made do with blankets on the floor. The following day the big clean up began and their trunk arrived so they were able to settle in properly. Rev.Mother Ligouri stayed a month to help set up the foundation but Sr.Magdalen set off back to Derby after a week.

They immediately started the works of the Congregation in this first rural foundation, whose needs Mother Augustine must have found very different from those of Derby. They visited the sick and poor and they gave Religious Instruction on Sundays.

Two weeks after their arrival the first of many postulants Jane Greene entered. As numbers increased new buildings were required. The Sisters had no cell accommodation, only improvised dormitories. The downstairs rooms acted as sleeping quarters by night and community room and parlour by day. The first addition made to the little Convent consisted of cells, community room, refectory and kitchen.

A bazaar was held in 1868 to help defray the expenses of the first school building. Others were held in the following years to help with other building projects and in aid of the poor. Soon there was a House of Mercy, an Orphanage, schools and a branch house in Thurles, Co.Tipperary.

The joy of the Sisters' early years' in Doon was tempered with sadness at the untimely deaths of a number of young Sisters. To balance this loss the community was blest with many vocations. Within two years the Community had doubled in size and by 1877 they were twenty-three in number. Sister de Pazzi and Sister Teresa returned to Kinsale in 1873 because, according to the Annals, "The Doon Community had grown so much". In 1887 there were over thirty Sisters and in 1899 they numbered over forty Sisters. A century after its foundation nearly a hundred Sisters working in six Convents. As well as getting postulants for their home convents, Doon also sent young girls to convents all over the world. Research carried out in the centenary year 1965, revealed that Doon school had produced two hundred and ninety six religious vocations – a record to be proud of. One of RTE's first documentary programmes in 1962 was a Radharc Programme on "The Parish with the most Religious Vocations in Ireland – Doon, Co.Limerick".

Over the years the Doon school sent many girls to Kinsale as postulants. Presently there are four members of the Kinsale Community who got their secondary education in Doon – Sr. Peter Ryan, Sr.Finbarr Morrissey, Sr.Agnes Beary and Sister Mary McAuliffe.

A strong bond existed between the Kinsale Sisters and the Doon Sisters. When the foundation was developing the Kinsale Rev.Mother and Sisters visited annually, but as the years went by the visits became less frequent. These visits of course were reciprocated. The two Fallon sisters – Sr.Evangelist, a pioneer of Skibbereen and Sr.Teresa a pioneer of Doon - often met in Kinsale.

Ballyshannon, Co. Donegal
St. Catherine's 1867

In his will dated November 21st 1849, Mr. William Stephens, a pious gentleman from Ballyshannon, made a bequest of one acre of land to bear a shilling a year rent which he intended as a site for the foundation of a Convent of Mercy in the town. He also left £1,150 towards the building and the establishment of this Convent.

The Bishop of Raphoe, Rev.Daniel McGettigan, visited Kinsale as early as 1865 to discuss the possibility of a foundation. Rev.Mother Ligouri and Mother Francis visited Ballyshannon in 1866 to make arrangements for the proposed foundation. With the negotiations completed and the securing of a house by the good bishop the foundation became a reality on April 30th 1867. The new Community consisted of Sr.Ignatius McCarthy who was to be Superior, Sr.de Sales Kelly, Sr.Borgia Hurley, Sr.Veronica Reardon and Sr.Agatha Shiel, (who had entered for the Ballyshannon foundation but unfortunately had to leave two years later due to illness). Rev.Mother Ligouri and Sr.Augustine Carroll accompanied the little band of pioneers who left Kinsale on April 26th. They stopped off in Baggot St. for a few days where the kind Bishop McGettigan met them and accompanied them to Ballyshannon. They arrived on the feast of St.Catherine of Siena, April 30th so the Convent was dedicated to this Saint and named St.Catherine's Convent of Mercy. The Bishop had everything ready for them on their arrival. The adjoining buildings were prepared as schools which opened on May 13th 1867.

The Sisters immediately started the visitation of the sick and poor in their homes. There was no hospital in the town only the Workhouse. A Sunday school for boys and girls was opened and the Sodalities for children, young boys and girls as well as men and women, were built up gradually.

Mother Ligouri and Sr.Augustine remained with the fledgling Community for the customary month to help establish the foundation.

The first postulant, Sarah Duncan from County Westmeath, joined the Community on December 12th 1867. She made her profession on St.Patricks Day 1870. Sadly she died eight years later, aged thirty-one. Other young girls continued to join the Community, and by April 1884 six new Sisters had arrived. Several of these died of consumption which was at that time rampant in Ireland. The damp and unhealthy conditions of their first Convent, which was susceptible to flooding caused much concern to Mother Ignatius. In spite of lacking the necessary funds a site was purchased and work began on the building of the new Convent. The Convent was eventually built having caused great stress and anxiety to the Superior. It had been halted for a while due to lack of funds. The people of the town had been very generous, but Mother Ignatius found it necessary to appeal to Irish Emigrants in America and Australia. The response to this appeal enabled the building to continue. The poverty and hardship caused by the partial famine of 1879 may well have been a factor in the deaths at the Convent.

In spite of the hardship the Sisters were experiencing they managed to establish the House of Mercy and the Orphanage. The new Convent opened in 1883. In 1890 the Sisters took control of the Workhouse. The Industrial School opened shortly afterwards. . Mother Ignatius' health declined and she died on May 17th 1888, nineteen years after arriving in Ballyshannon. Sr.deSales, Sr.Borgia and Sr.Veronica had previously returned to Kinsale.

In 1890 the Sisters expanded to Glenties where they opened a Primary School.

In 1894 they took charge of the new Shiel Hospital. Doctor Simon Shiel Junior, a brother of Agatha Shiel who joined Kinsale Convent for the Ballyshannon Mission, left £6,000 in his will towards the building of this hospital for the sick of the area. It is interesting to note that Agatha was herself generous to the Sisters in her will.

The Community prospered and radiated out from Ballyshannon taking over St.Patricks Workhouse in Glenties in 1898 and St.Joseph's Workhouse in Stranorlar in 1899. The Donegal Primary School opened in 1905, and in 1919 Carrickboy Primary School was established. Second Level Education in the care of the Sisters of Mercy began in Ballyshannon in 1947. As well as the great expansion taking place at home, Convents of Mercy all around Donegal were commonplace by the middle of this century. The Sisters went to Billings, Montana, in 1966 and to St.Luke's Parish Great Falls, also in Montana, in 1977.

There are strong links between Convent of Mercy, Kinsale and St.Catherine's, Ballyshannon. Following the founding Sisters the first Kinsale girl to depart for Ballyshannon was Sr.Kevin Carroll in 1933. There are five Kinsale "girls" ministering in the Diocese of Raphoe today – Sr.Carmel Kiernan, Sr.Immaculata Coughlan, Sr.Concepta Murphy, Sr.Stella Herlihy and Sr.Mary O'Donovan.

St. Vincent Ferrer
Delray Beach, Florida 1955

Delray Beach, Florida written about in Chapter One is the only foundation of the twentieth century. The Sisters were invited to go there in 1954 - exactly one hundred years after the intrepid Mercy pioneers headed for California - to staff the new parochial school being built at St.Vincent Ferrer Parish. From among the many Sisters who volunteered for this mission the chosen four were Sr.Baptist Molloy, Sr.Albert Treacy, Sr.Teresita O'Shea and Sr.Peter Ryan. They set sail from Cobh on the "S.S. America" on August 10th 1955. They arrived in Palm Beach on August 25th where Father Kellaghan and a group of parishioners welcomed them. They were taken to their new temporary home – the rectory while the kind Fr.Kellaghan moved out to an apartment to accommodate them. Since the school was not yet finished and the Sisters were eager to begin work, they taught the children in the living and dining room of the rectory. Their new school opened on October 25th 1955.

Sr.Teresita O'Shea is the sole survivor of the original group who left Kinsale in 1955. Sr.Baptist Molloy and Sr.Albert Treacy have both died and Sr.Peter Ryan has returned to Kinsale. Other Sisters have joined the mission over the years and now Sr.Teresita O'Shea, Sr.Finbarr Morrissey and Sr.Clare Fennel continue to labour there.

Delray Beach Community celebrating the Silver Jubilee of their Foundation

Back: left to right
Sr Finbarr Morrissey, the late Sr. Bernard Millett, the late Sr. Baptist Molloy, the late Sr. Albert Treacy

Front: left to right
Sr. Clare Fennell, Sr. Teresite O'Shea, Sr Peter Ryan

By their deeds we shall know them.

This is indeed an impressive legacy. I feel privileged to have been chosen to "make their deeds known." Due to this era of expansion, Mercy has taken root firmly all over the world and become one of the largest and well-known Congregations within the Church.

When you next visit Kinsale sit on the seat erected on the pier by the past pupils to commemorate the 150th anniversary of the foundation of the Kinsale convent. The list of the above foundations is written on top of the seat.

"O commemorate me

where there is water,

Canal bank water preferably, so

Stilly greeny at the heart of summer

Just a canal-bank seat,

for the passer by"

(P. Kavanagh.)

Chapter 3
Pioneering Women

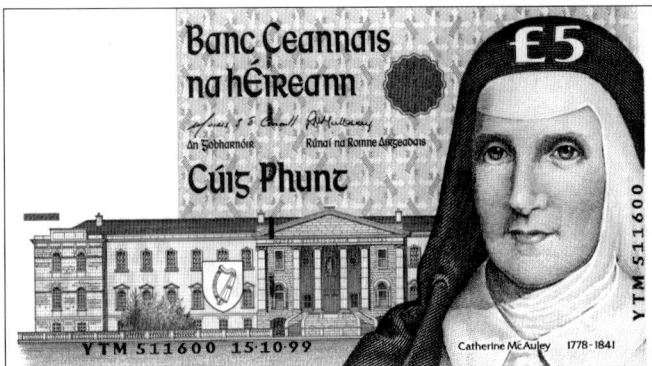

Mother C. C McAuley honoured by the Central Bank

Catherine McAuley
Foundress of the Sisters of Mercy

Catherine McAuley was born on September 29th 1778 at Stormanston House in North County Dublin. She was the eldest child of James and Elinor McAuley. James McAuley even though a Catholic was a well to do builder, which was quite unusual for that time in Ireland. Although James died when Catherine was only five years old, his great love and compassion for the poor, who were always made welcome and fed at Stormanston House, stayed with Catherine for the rest of her life.

Her mother was devastated by the death of her husband and since she was unable to manage the family's affairs they soon became quite poor.

After her mother's death in 1798, Catherine who was twenty went to live with her uncle Owen Conway and his daughter, Ann. Her sister, Mary, and her brother, James, went to live with Protestant relatives, the Armstrongs, who lived close by, so they were able to see each other regularly.

Catherine liked living with the Conways. She and Ann were very close. They begged clothes, curtains, etc. from their wealthy friends and neighbours, and with the help of their friends made clothes for the poor. They also took food to the poor. Catherine was able to practise her Catholic faith without fear of ridicule. Her brother and sister gave up their practice while living with the Armstrongs who were Protestant.

Unfortunately the Conways went bankrupt, so Catherine and Ann experienced real poverty themselves. The O'Callaghans, an elderly couple who had recently returned from India, met Catherine at the home of the Armstrongs and were so impressed with her that they invited her to live with them at Coolock House. The O'Callaghans, who were Quakers, were very supportive of Catherine's work for the poor but did not approve of her Catholic Faith.

Catherine spent twenty years with the O'Callaghans at Coolock House, where she gave Religious instruction to the poor children of the area as well as the household servants. She taught needlework to young women and set up a little shop where they could sell their wares.

When the O'Callaghans died - both of whom had embraced the Catholic faith on their deathbeds - they left their considerable fortune to Catherine, knowing that she would use it wisely to provide "protection and education for young servant girls".

Some of these servant girls were very badly treated, and Catherine had already taken an interest in them and had hoped one day to have a house where they could receive shelter.

Catherine was very sad at the loss of the O'Callaghans, who had been a second father and mother to her. In spite of all the grief she experienced in her life, she never lost sight of her goals and never faltered in her care of the poor and the oppressed.

The fortune she inherited enabled Catherine to realise her plan to educate young girls and also to extend her vision to a variety of social services for poor women and children.

In 1824 she was able to buy a site in the fashionable Baggot Street area of Dublin which became known as "Kitty's Folly" by her family. They did not approve of her plan to bring the wealthy people of the Baggot St. area into contact with the plight of the poor. Her hope was that some of the privileged people of this area would support or even join in her service.

While the property was being built she studied educational methods in Ireland and in France and became an instructor in one of the Poor Schools.Many people thought she was crazy squandering her vast fortune on the poor and needy instead of indulging herself, travelling and socialising.

Again tragedy struck; her sister Mary became seriously ill. Catherine cared for her and her five children until she died; then she took on the legal guardianship of her nieces and nephews, their father already being dead.

The house in Baggot St. opened on September 24th 1827, the feast of Our Lady of Mercy, so it was placed under the patronage of the Mother of Mercy. It contained a school, a shelter for homeless girls and a home for orphaned children.

The House of Mercy flourished and hundreds of girls enrolled in the school. Many young girls offered themselves as helpers. There were about twelve women living at Baggot St. in the early days. The visitation of the sick was also added to their activities. Catherine, having sold Coolock House, moved into Baggot St. in June 1828.

As time went by the women began to dress similarly and simply, live by a regular timetable and call each other sister. Even though Catherine had no notion of becoming a nun or founding a convent the question of her status became an issue. She agreed to the establishment of a Religious Order only when she was assured that she and her companions could continue with their work.

On September 8th1830 Catherine and two companions went to the Presentation Convent in George's Hill, Dublin, to begin their noviciate. She was fifty-two years old.

Fifteen months later, on December 12th 1831, they were professed. On that wonderful day the Congregation of Our Lady of Mercy was born.

Before her death, ten years later, Catherine had founded fourteen Convents of Mercy in Ireland and England. The Sisters of Mercy became known as "Walking Nuns" as they were often seen out in the homes of the poor or the sick. Nuns were mostly enclosed at that time. Many young girls, including Catherine's own niece, joined them in those early days. Each new foundation was independent of the Mother House. Catherine went herself to each new foundation and stayed to help set up its ministry and lead the Sisters in prayer. Even though the Convents were independent she kept in touch with them and linked them together with frequent visits and letters. In June 1841 there were 142 Sisters of Mercy. The Pope approved of the Congregation of the Sisters of Mercy as a Religious Congregation.

The Convent of Mercy Limerick, which has particular significance for Kinsale, as St.Joseph's was founded from there, was established in 1836.

Catherine travelled around a great deal in those years and was continuously busy setting the congregation on a sure footing. This took its toll. In September 1841 she returned from Birmingham, really ill, and was carried to the infirmary. She was dying of T.B. and in terrific pain and died on November 11th of that year. Before her death she instructed those who were caring for her "to give the Sisters a cup of tea when I go".

Catherine had a magnetic personality. She was gentle and charming, full of fun and loved to dance. She often sent her letters out in verse form.

Mother Mary Anne Burke
Kinsale

Ellen Foley McNamara, daughter of Belinda Foley and John McNamara, was born in Macroom in 1796. Sadly, very little is known about this very important figure in the Kinsale story. Clearly she came from a wealthy family judging from her beautiful furniture and silver, adorning St.Joseph's, Kinsale.

She married Michael Burke, about whom we know nothing. Unfortunately he died shortly after the marriage, and when her time of mourning was over she expressed a desire to enter a Religious Congregation and to use her considerable wealth to help found a Convent in her native Macroom.

The Irish Sisters of Charity, founded by the Cork lady Mother Mary Aikenhead, was her first choice. In 1841 while on her way to Dublin in the company of her brother, Father Justin Foley McNamara Parish Priest of Kinsale, she visited St.Mary's Convent of Mercy, Limerick. Ellen was very impressed by the story they told her about Catherine McAuley and her new Congregation. Even though she continued on to Dublin and joined the Sisters of Charity, Gardner St., her heart was in Limerick with the Sisters of Mercy. After some months she left

Gardner St. and joined the Mercy Congregation in Limerick on July 31st 1841, with a view to founding a convent in Kinsale. Her persuasive brother had convinced her that Kinsale's need was greater than Macroom's, it being a garrison town. On December 12th 1843 Ellen, known now as Sr.Mary Anne Joseph Burke, made her first profession. She was a lady of many virtues and possessed a sweet disposition. Before she entered the Convent she was renowned for her generosity to the poor and needy, and she never missed an opportunity to try and redeem a lost soul. According to the Annals of St.Mary's Limerick "Her great attraction was drawing people from habits of sin, and knowing her position in society, she never feared to lose it by speaking to a poor lost one - even in the public street - whom she knew and who very evidently shrank from meeting her after having fallen from virtue, to try and induce her to return to the path of rectitude." She was often criticised for mixing with people of "low morals" and often her friends, fearing for her reputation, would complain to her brother, Fr.Justin: "Do you know to whom I saw your sister speaking in the street the other day?"

She was a most unselfish person, kind and loving towards her fellow Sisters. On visitation to the homes of the poor and sick she was "sweet, devoted and earnest" according to the Limerick annals. She endeavoured to make the children under her care in school good and pious. In fact it has been said that her many qualities outweighed the wealth she gave for the promotion of God's work. A humble woman, Mother Mary Anne, never sought to promote herself and was always happier to play a supporting role to the more dynamic Mother Francis Bridgeman. She was forty eight years old when she came as foundress to Kinsale and for most of that time she was Mother Assistant, firstly to Mother Francis and then to Mother Teresa Maher. Her gentle presence helped lay the deep spiritual foundations which support the community to this day. She aided the growth and development of the Works of Mercy in the town, witnessed the departure of so many Sisters to distant foundations, and like Mary she "pondered all these things in her heart." She died on March 22nd 1870, aged seventy-four years, having borne patiently a long and painful illness. Her Superior wrote, "...Charity was her leading virtue. In her the Community lost a holy, loving mother and a bright example of every virtue." She took as her motto "In Thee, O Lord, have I hoped" - we know she was not disappointed.

Mother Francis Bridgeman
Kinsale and The Crimea

Joanna, daughter of Hewitt and Marianne Bridgeman from Ballagh, Ruan, Co.Clare was born in 1815.

She entered St.Mary's Convent of Mercy, Limerick, on September 24th 1838. Her Novitiate was made in Baggot St. where she had the good fortune to come under the direct influence of Catherine McAuley. Mother McAuley officiated at her reception, which was indeed a red-letter day for the Mercy Congregation.

Being a gifted but humble person, who had known tragedy in her young life, she found the Noviatiate difficult. Her parents died at a young age and her aunt, Joanna Reddan whom Joanna and her brothers loved, had brought them up. It was painful for Joanna to be separated from those she loved. We shall read about her aunt later in this chapter.

The young Joanna had helped Miss Reddan attend to cholera patients, teach in a Poor School and run a Magdalen Asylum in Limerick.

Mother Francis was appointed first Superior to the new Mercy Convent in Kinsale. She worked tirelessly to establish the foundation and to develop the works of Mercy in the town. She it was who in the spirit of her foundress Catherine McAuley sent young Sisters off on Foundations far and wide, making sure, like any good parent, that they were well provided for. They went with confidence knowing the home Community was holding them in their prayers.

Mother Francis' greatest challenge came in 1854. It was the call to nurse the soldiers in the Crimea. The situation in the Crimea was so desperate that the Sisters of Mercy were requested by Monsignor Grant of Southwark to send some sisters to help nurse the soldiers. He thought it might help the soldiers to be nursed by English speaking nuns.

Her experience in Limerick and at the Kinsale Workhouse during the 1849 cholera outbreak, as well as her personal qualities of organization and zeal, made Mother Francis the obvious choice to lead the party of fifteen Sisters chosen for this difficult faraway mission. Two other Sisters from Kinsale formed part of this extraordinary group, Sister Joseph Lynch, who later blazed a Mercy trail across America and Sr.Clare Keane renowned for her holiness. Sisters Agnes Whitty and Elizabeth Hersey from Baggot St., Sisters Paula Rice and Aloysius Hurley from Cork, Sisters Joseph Croke and Clare Lalor from Charleville, Sisters Aloysius Doyle and Stanislaus Hefron from Carlow, Sisters Elizabeth Butler, Winefrede Sprey and Magdalen Alcock from Liverpool and Sister Bernard Dixon from Chelsea completed the group of Mercy Sisters. Mother Francis won the hearts and confidence of these Sisters for her warm motherly care of them. They considered her to have the "most captivating manner". Sister Aloysius Doyle who wrote her own account of her time in the Crimea and who lived until 1908, refers to her as "Our Eastern Mother" and says, "I loved her the minute I saw her."

The Sisters were badly received by the British Authorities who looked on them as inferior beings on two counts: they were Irish and they were Catholic.

The entire Nursing Party consisted of ten ladies in the care of Miss Stanley daughter of the Anglican Archbishop of Norwich and a colleague of Florence Nightingale, twenty-three paid nurses, and the fifteen Sisters. They travelled by French steamer with about 300 soldiers. The journey was a difficult one and they were ill on the journey from Dublin because of rough seas. They spent a night in London where they met up with the other members of the group. A weekend was spent in Paris from where they travelled by train to Lyons and by steamer down the Rhone to Valence where their boat struck a sandbank. This delayed their arrival in Marseille. From here they went on the "Egyptus," a rickety unseaworthy mail boat. The ladies of the party were allocated cabins but the Sisters had to travel steerage, with the nurses who behaved badly on the trip causing embarrassment to the Sisters. When they ran into stormy weather the Sisters found their berths swamped, and their trunks covered in four feet of water. Their bedding and personal belongings were floating in the water. Mother Francis by now had won the admiration of the lady volunteers and the respect of the hired nurses. Sister Stanislaus Hefron said, "indeed anyone would like her." She is reputed to have had a heart as well as a head- a most capable and able woman. When the party finally reached Constantinople, Florence Nightingale who claimed that their arrival "had been a gross misunderstanding on the part of the War Office" and that there was neither employment nor accommodation for them in the hospitals, gave them a very frosty reception. This was at times when between fifty and ninety men were dying daily in Scutari! She then assigned the Sisters to non-nursing jobs, such as cleaning out cupboards and insisted that they were not to go near the patients. The chaplain, Fr.Ronan S.J. informed Miss Nightingale that he would take the Sisters home if they were not allowed to do what their contract permitted them to do. This changed matters. Why would nurses be returning home when the British publics were still reading in "The Times" how desperately nurses were needed?

Mother Francis Bridgeman and her Sisters, who were among the best-prepared nurses of the nineteenth century, were denied access to the hospitals and the sick. When Mother Francis confronted Miss Nightingale on behalf of the Sisters, she agreed to provide nursing services to all soldiers and confine spiritual counselling to Catholics only. She would be in charge of the nuns who in matters of nursing would serve under Florence Nightingale.

This war is better remembered for its glaring military blunders than for its solution to any problems, which existed but then of course war is never a solution.

This war was about territory. Under Catherine the Great, Russia gained much new territory including the Crimean Peninsula in the Ukraine on the Black Sea. With the defeat of Napoleon in 1815, Russia was the great military power in Europe, and it wanted now to extend into the Balkans which was ruled by the Ottomans. Russia did not like the fact that the Ottomans controlled the Bosphorous and the Dardanelles.

Britain and France resented Russia's attempt to gain land from the Ottomans, so when Russia invaded Turkish territory in 1853 Britain and France went to the aid of the Ottomans attacking Russia on the Crimean Peninsula. The war lasted from October 1853 until February 1856, and the Russians were defeated. There was huge loss of life in this conflict, but it is said that as many died of cholera as did, as a result of the war. Lord Cardigan's misunderstanding of his Commander's instructions led to the deaths of two hundred and forty seven men out of a force of six hundred and seventy- three, made famous by Alfred Lord Tennyson in his poem "The Charge of The Light Brigade", verse two of which is quoted here.

"Forward, the Light Brigade!

Was there man dismay'd?

Not tho' the soldier knew

Someone had blunder'd:

Their's not to make reply,

Their's not to reason why,

Their's but to do and die:

Into the valley of Death

Rode the six hundred."

W.H. Russell, an Irish journalist, the first war correspondent in history, by his use of the telegraph got information quickly back to his Editor at the "London Times". His graphic eyewitness accounts made the British public critical of the war and the plight of their soldiers who were dying for no good reason so far from home.

The Sisters worked long and hard in the most awful conditions to alleviate the suffering of the unfortunate soldiers, one third of whom were Irish recruits. Two Sisters from Liverpool died of cholera, a cause of great sadness to the little band of Mercy who were suffering so much hardship already, both from the authorities and from Florence Nightingale who was in charge of the nurses. Florence disliked Mother Francis and referred to her disrespectfully as "Mother Brickbat" or "Rev.Brickbat" They had many skirmishes. Authority to Miss Nightingale, it appears, meant power while to Mother Francis it meant service. There were times too of peaceful relations between them. Florence showed her own generosity of spirit, on the death of Sister Winefrede, she offered to erect a headstone to her memory, and in a letter to Sidney Herbert at the war office she declared that "The Rev.Brickbat and I are the best of friends". It is inappropriate that we form harsh judgements on any of the players in this tragedy since we do not know what effect the situation, the conditions and the futility of it all had on them. Certainly Mother Francis and Florence Nightingale were strong personalities; perhaps a clash was inevitable.

Conditions for the Sisters in the Crimea were appalling. Their quarters were unfurnished, apart from a backless chair! There was no heating and no cooking facilities, so the poor Sisters could not even make a cup of tea. The windows were without glass, just imagine in the cold of a Russian winter. They were eventually put in charge of the Turkish Barracks which had been turned into a hospital. There were thousands of sick and wounded, lying here in the most pitiful conditions, no heating and poor food. Drinking water was scarce and there was no water for washing. The place was alive with vermin. The huge rats had consumed much of the bedding and clothing. The air was putrid with the smell of bodies which had not been properly buried.

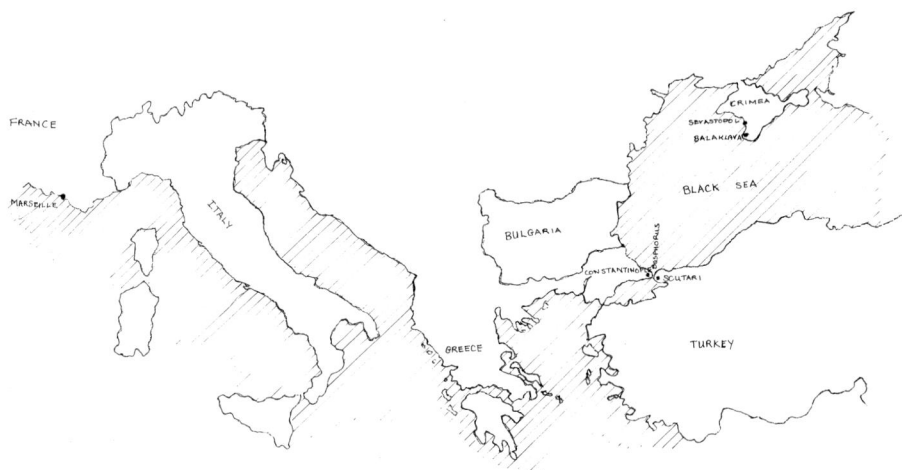

The Sisters gained the respect of one and all for their care of the sick and suffering. *"They were never surprised, never put out, meeting all difficulties with a cheerful spirit"* - according to an article in the "North British Review".

In another book "Eastern Hospitals and English Nurses" we find further praise *"The superiority of the Catholic Sisters of Mercy showed itself over all other classes of nurses engaged in the East. To them the care of the sick and the suffering was no new thing undertaken in the heat of enthusiasm."* The Sisters worked for no payment in the Crimea. They received a donation of £250 for the poor whom they cared for in Ireland. The English public raised £50,000 in recognition of Florence Nightingale's service. With this she founded a home for training nurses.

There is no mention of the contribution of the Sisters of Mercy in the histories of the Crimean

War, but I have no doubt that they lived forever in the hearts of the soldiers whom they cared for so lovingly in this far away place.

Mother Francis rarely spoke of her experiences in the East, and her advice to all concerned was "Whatever you say, say nothing". We can only speculate as to what her observations were of this catastrophe which was to take the lives of so many soldiers and the two dear Sisters from Liverpool who did not come home.

On their way home from the Crimea the three Kinsale Sisters called at the Derby foundation. The three priests of the town, Canon Sing, Canon Daniel and Fr.Gogarty met them at the station and conducted them to the Convent in a carriage drawn by four grey horses. Soldiers were arranged at either side of the Convent entrance and the Sisters received a right royal welcome in recognition of their services to their comrades in the Crimea. Crowds of spectators came to cheer the Sisters.

When they returned to Kinsale they made their way quietly to their Convent home managing to side step the celebrations the town had planned in their honour. The whole experience no doubt left a lasting impression which they hardly regarded as a cause for celebration. They settled back into Community life and continued the work they had been called to do. Fr.Ronan S.J. a good friend to the Sisters and especially to Mother Francis, became a regular visitor to Kinsale until his death. He said of Mother Francis that *"he had never met any one with a mind like hers, yet she was so simple she would learn from a child."* Another friend whom they met in the Crimea was Fanny Taylor, daughter of an Anglican Vicar. Through her friendship with the Sisters she became a Catholic and on her return to London founded the Congregation of the Poor Servants of the Mother of God. She retained a lifelong friendship with the Kinsale Community.

Mother Francis' contribution to education is still evident in her work "God in His Ways".

She served the Community as Superior every alternate six years until her death on February 11th 1888. These were years of progress and expansion. Mother Francis continued to guide and help the foundations she sent out until they were able to manage their own affairs; then she was happy to "let them go" while still being available to them should they need her advice.

She took a terrific interest in the day to day running of the schools, the hospital, the orphanage or the workroom, all of which gained from her amazing administrative skills.

She was seen regularly visiting the homes of the poor and the sick. Always cheerful and light-hearted, she brought sunshine into their sad lives. She, like her role model Catherine McAuley, "would willingly suffer want herself rather than see God's poor neglected".

Being among the young was of particular delight to her, and as she grew older she would often be seen sitting surrounded by little ones, some sitting on her lap, others attached to her shawl hanging on her every word as she simplified the catechism for them and rewarded them with sweets from her deep pockets.

A malignant growth caused her great pain, which she bore patiently until she died peacefully, surrounded by her grieving Community on February 11th 1888.

Tributes flowed into St.Joseph's following her death, and the "Tablet" in its issue dated February 20th 1888 published an article entitled "The Nun in the Crimea" giving an account of her achievements.

The most laudable tribute of all came from a Jesuit priest - Father Michael Duffy - who knew her in the Crimea: *"We were fellow soldiers there, under the same flag - Christ's - and it belongs to fellow soldiers to help each other in the hour of need. Not that she has any great need, after her long service in the 'King's' cause. Therefore it is not the "De Profundis" that I shall sing for her, but rather a "Te Deum Laudamus"!"*

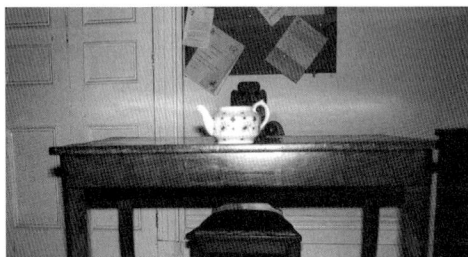

"Teapot" - Souvenir of Crimea.
The Table which travelled to the Crimea and back serving as a "trunk" can be seen in the Community Room

Mother Evangelist Benson
Derby

Sister Evangelist Benson, daughter of William and Margaret Benson was born in Dublin in 1812. She entered St.Joseph's Kinsale in 1845 one year after its foundation. Clearly she was a talented lady because four years later she was chosen as leader of the first foundation. Dr.Ullathorne, the Bishop of the Midland District, confirmed her appointment as Reverend Mother of the Derby Convent of Mercy on November 10th 1849.

On her arrival Mother Evangelist seemed to be of delicate health, but she seemed to gain in strength and courage and the foundation flourished.

Long before Aneurin Bevan introduced the "Welfare State" Mother Evangelist and her Sisters worked in every area of deprivation and spearheaded Catholic Education in the British

Midlands. Mother Evangelist guided the community wisely and well for forty years until her death on July 6th 1889. From the beginning she had been a devoted mother to her community, and they loved her deeply. She was highly esteemed by all who knew her.

Mother Joseph Lynch
Crimea and USA

Alicia Lynch was the daughter of Timothy and Sarah Lynch who owned a greengrocer shop near St.Finbarrs, South Parish in Cork. She was one of many children. We know that four other members of her family emigrated to America. She was tall, attractive and very talented, a good organiser, intelligent, independent and very straightforward. She was the first postulant to enter the newly established Convent of Mercy at Kinsale, arriving on May 8th 1844, less than a month after its opening. She was professed on December 8th 1846. No doubt she was actively involved in the setting up of the works of Mercy in Kinsale.

She accompanied Mother Francis Bridgeman and the founding sisters to Derby in October 1849 to set up the first Convent of Mercy there.

Later, in October 1854, she was chosen to go to the Crimea, where she remained for sixteen months. Her friend, Sr.Clare Keane, became quite ill during their time in the Crimea where they endured terrific hardship nursing cholera patients.

She was by now quite an experienced "pioneer", full of missionary zeal and years ahead of her time. She was a competent teacher and very skilful in the care of the sick and of course had gained tremendous experience in the early days in Kinsale.

When a priest visited Kinsale seeking Sisters for the Convent of Mercy, Brooklyn, New York, off she went. According to the annals "She went of her own free will". The Chapter consented to same on 30th October 1859. No member of the community accompanied her". Strangely, it was stipulated that she would not be re-admitted to Kinsale even if she wanted to return. She was indeed a brave lady.

It is believed that she travelled to America with her brother. The Brooklyn Community was four years old when she joined them. She was an experienced administrator, and she was so highly esteemed by her new Community that in 1860, one year after her arrival she became their first Mother Assistant and also took on the duties of Bursar.

She was an energetic and hardworking woman and as bursar she set the community on a firm financial footing. She was responsible for the opening of the Industrial School and Orphanage in Brooklyn in 1862. Later she opened a school for fee-paying girls.

She worked so hard and with such zeal that she had health problems and asked for leave of absence.

She went to Rochester and set up an Industrial School. Having spent a year in Rochester the Brooklyn Community refused to have her back.

She was not phased by this. She set off for Grand Rapids Michigan, accompanied by three young novices. When they arrived at Grand Rapids there was nobody to meet them. A telegram had been sent advising them not to come, but as they had already set out they did not get the message. Local ladies rallied 'round, housing the Sisters until a Convent could be found. They started the works of Mercy there - visiting the sick and the poor and teaching the children.

Personality clashes with the Bishop and the Parish Priest, huge debts and no proper contract resulted in the Sisters being in dire straits. At that time the parishes did not seem to be able to support the Sisters. They seemed to think that the Sisters had independent means and did not need to be supported while they gave their all in the care of the sick, poor and ignorant.

Leaving Mother Alphonsus Thileman in charge in Grand Rapids, Mother Mary Joseph Lynch moved to Big Rapids which was a lumberjack community. The Parish Priest promised the Sisters a house for themselves and a hospital and school for their apostolate. The lumbermen had already started collecting for the hospital. The P.P. was not very vigilant about his financial accounting and had assumed the Bishop's approval for asking the Sisters to come there. The Bishop seemed to have some problem with Mother Joseph and her little band. He said they were not a "proper" Religious Community!

Soon they had their house and a very primitive hospital, but due to further conflict with the bishop, who regarded her as a fraud, Mother Joseph had to move on again to another diocese.

She spent the years from 1879 until 1896 in Minnesota, firstly in Mendota where she opened an Industrial School and a day school. Mendota was too small for the growing Religious Community, so the Sisters moved to nearby Anoka where they were given the gift of a large residence.

Mother Joseph then moved on to Minneapolis where a fine hospital named after the Mater Misericordiae in Dublin was built. Again she was beset by troubles - lacking money for expansion. The Bishop seemed to have some prejudice against the Sisters of Mercy. He also hated getting into debt so he asked Mother Joseph to find another diocese. In 1885 she moved on to Morris where the Sisters received no help from the parish for their school. Parents who could afford it paid a small monthly tuition fee for their children.

The Sisters managed to get a 240-acre farm where they built an Industrial School for the education of Indian children. Mother Joseph solicited money from all and sundry for her projects with these children. She sent samples of their handcraft to the World Fair in Chicago in 1893 where it was much praised and won several blue ribbons.

The Community had grown to twenty-four Sisters and in 1896 the Bishop asked them to move to Oregon. He wanted them to start a home for working girls in Portland, Oregon,

so Mother Joseph and seven other Sisters went West by train on the newly opened railroad. The journey took three days. On arriving in Portland they opened a home for working girls and a home for the aged.

 Mother Joseph was growing tired. She had blazed a trail of Mercy across the USA being constantly at the cutting edge, and of course it was taking its toll on her health.

While her Community was preparing for the celebration of her Golden Jubilee, she was stranded in Wyoming in a snowstorm, which blocked the tracks. The celebration took place without her!

The Community had to beg for funds until they could become self-supporting. Music lessons were another source of income and they took sewing classes also.

At Christmas 1897 Mother Joseph Lynch caught a cold from which she never recovered. She died peacefully on May 19th 1898.

She had devoted fifty-four years to bringing Mercy wheresoever she found herself. Her zeal for the spreading of the congregation was without question. Most of the places she struggled in are flourishing Mercy Communities today. We owe her a great debt of gratitude.

Kinsale reminiscences depict her as "capable, clever, charming - but a character apart."

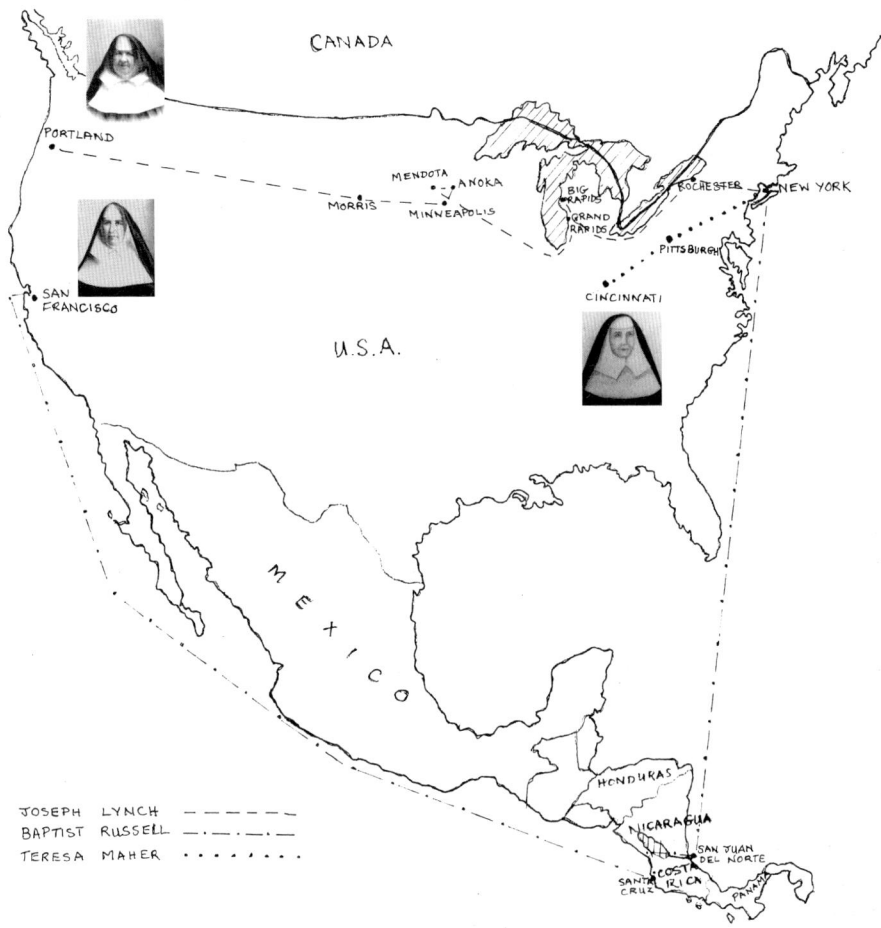

CANADA

PORTLAND

MENDOTA
ANOKA
MORRIS
MINNEAPOLIS

BIG
RAPIDS
GRAND
RAPIDS

ROCHESTER
NEW YORK

PITTSBURGH

SAN
FRANCISCO

U.S.A.

CINCINNATI

M E X I C O

JOSEPH   LYNCH   — — — — —
BAPTIST RUSSELL — . — . — . —
TERESA   MAHER   · · · · ✦ · · ·

HONDURAS

NICARAGUA

SAN JUAN
DEL NORTE

COSTA
RICA

SANTA
CRUZ

PANAMA

Mother Baptist Russell
San Francisco

The extraordinary life of Katherine Russell began in Newry, Co.Down where she was born on August 18th 1829, shortly after the winning of Catholic Emancipation. Her mother Margaret Mullan from Belfast, married the wealthy merchant John Hamill when she was seventeen years old. He died twelve years later leaving her with six young children, three boys and three girls.

Five years later, in January 1825 she married the dashing ship's captain, Arthur Russell, from Killough, a small fishing port in Co.Down about five miles from Downpatrick.

The Russells had been planted in Northern Ireland in the twelfth century. They were one of the families who did not change their religion with Henry V111. Arthur retired from the sea and bought a brewery in Newry, and the family moved to 50 Queen Street where Katherine, her sisters and brothers were born. Arthur and Margaret had four daughters and two sons. Mary, their eldest daughter who died at the age of thirteen, Elizabeth, Katherine, Sarah, Charles and Matthew. Their five surviving children excelled themselves in their chosen way of life.

Charles, born in 1832 became the first Catholic Lord Chief Justice of England since the Reformation. He won fame as Gladstone's Attorney General and was regarded the finest advocate of his age. He was knighted for his brilliant services in representing Britain against the United States in the Bering Sea controversy in 1893 - A dispute Britain and Canada had with the USA over the International status of the Bering Sea. When in 1894 Queen Victoria granted him a life peerage, he took the title Lord Russell of Killowen to distinguish himself from the other Lord Russells.

Matthew became a Jesuit priest renowned for his oratory and his writings of his family history - "The three Sisters of Lord Russell" and "Life of Mother Baptist Russell."

The three girls became Sisters of Mercy. All became Foundresses of new Convents. We shall read of Elizabeth and Sarah later in this chapter.

Katherine and her sisters and brothers went to a private primary school. When she was nine years old her father's health began to fail. The family bought a sixteen-acre estate with a lovely rambling old house in Killowen on Carlingford Lough, where her father could benefit from the fresh air. The children had a governess while they lived here and were taught, French, botany, astronomy, art, music, philosophy, and geology as well the more usual subjects, history, English, etc.

When Arthur Russell died in 1845 the family moved back to their home in Newry - 50 Queen Street. Katherine and her sisters went to finishing school. Even though they were a highly privileged family they were not unaware of the poverty and misery that surrounded them during the famine that was raging at this time. Along with the famine there was fever and disease sweeping through the country. The Russell children while well cared for were never overindulged. They had few toys or luxuries. Their mother trained the children to serve people who were in need. She never gave expensive dinner parties but gave generously to charity. All of the children had to do their share of the household chores and had to read aloud a chapter from the Bible after Sunday lunch. Mrs. Russell also handed over the responsibility for running the household to each of her daughters in turn. They had to make sure that everybody was fed and cared for and all the bills paid. This was certainly very good training for them and showed how much confidence she had in their abilities. No wonder they became such good managers of Communities during their lives as Sisters of Mercy.

Katherine as a teenager helped her mother with visiting and helping the starving poor of Newry. During this time she developed a great love for the poor and destitute.

When she was nineteen she asked permission to join the Sisters of Charity, but her mother suggested she join Mother McAuleys's "Walking Nuns" who were doing such wonderful work among the poor in the cities and towns of Ireland. The Sisters of Mercy was a fast growing Congregation full of zealous young women, and Mrs Russell felt it would be more suited to her talented young daughter. Katherine's uncle and guardian, Father Charles Russell president of Maynooth Diocesan College recommended that she join Mother Francis Bridgeman in Kinsale. On November 24th 1848 she entered the Convent of Mercy, Kinsale.

She is remembered as an attractive young girl with fair hair and rosy cheeks, full of fun and common sense. She was a wonderful friend. She could be approached with any difficulty and was willing to offer a ready solution. She also had boundless energy, so got through a great deal of work in the course of a day. She is remembered as being a very humble soul, and even as a novice she showed great charity to the other novices, always defending them to Mother Francis.

At her reception into the Mercy Order in 1849 she took the name Baptist. During this year she was called on to help the finally professed Sisters in their care of the cholera victims at the local workhouse. Her home training helped her here, and she showed great skill in caring for and comforting the sick and dying.

Sr.Baptist made her first profession on August 2nd 1851, and until her final profession in 1854 she got on with the job of teaching in the growing primary school in Kinsale, little knowing the great adventure that was ahead of her.

We have read in the previous chapter that she was chosen at the age of twenty- five to lead the foundation to San Francisco and of her remarkable journey to and extraordinary work in that city. She visited Kinsale in 1878 and entertained the community with tales of the city of St.Francis, which previously as an Indian Settlement had been known as "Yerba Bueno" - The Good Herb.

She spent forty-four years in the Far West shaping social institutions on the Pacific coast and extending the frontiers of the Catholic Faith. Roman Catholicism played a tremendous role in determining the life and culture of this new state.

Mother Baptist was renowned for her love of the poor. One day she gave away her hair mattress to a poor man whose need she said was greater than hers. She used to take things from the infirmary for the poor. The hospital linen room had to be kept locked otherwise she would "steal" all the linen for her precious poor!

She was named with nine men as one of the Founders of the city of San Francisco.

For the care and service the Sisters had given the city during the cholera outbreak Mother Baptist was asked by the rulers of the city to make a request to the city. Mother Baptist showed amazing foresight in asking for free travel around the city for all religious. To this day nuns may travel freely on the San Francisco transport system.

She was greatly saddened by the death of Mother De Sales Reddan who had been such a source of strength to her while establishing the foundation.

She led the Community through difficult and trying times, always shouldering the responsibility herself.

San Francisco's only hospital - The State Marine and County Hospital - was sited in Stockton St. opposite the Convent. At this time hospitals were just emerging from an era known as the "Dark Age of Nursing (1600 - 1850) during which overcrowding, filth, untrained nurses and lack of proper equipment made hospitals little better than jails". ("A Bulletin of American Hospitals" 1929). Many hospitals around the world were trying to improve their conditions but unfortunately this new trend had not reached California. William Taylor, a Methodist Minister, gives the following account of San Francisco's hospital: *"I thought the private rooms upstairs were filthy enough to kill any well man who would there confine himself, but in comparison with the others (public), they were entitled to be called choice rooms. The "lower wards" were so offensive to the eyes and especially to the olfactories that it was with great difficulty that I could remain long enough to do what I deemed my duty. The nurses were generally low men devoid of sympathy, careless, rude in the care of the sick, and exceedingly vulgar and profane."*

The Sisters of Mercy, led by Mother Baptist, changed all that when they took over the hospital on October 24th 1855. This started a Church-State relationship which was to have a backlash from the bigotry of the Know-Nothing-Party.

In 1856 the editor of the "San Francisco Daily Evening Bulletin" launched an invidious attack upon the Sisters' management of the hospital. . The Editor - James King of Williams was an unscrupulous man, who wrote sensational type editorials designed to arouse dangerously high feelings in the city. Unfortunately he did not know the difference between editorials and personal lying. Many of the charges he made could not be sustained by any proof. He sustained this attack in daily editorials for about eight weeks until one of the City Supervisors whom he had slandered -a man called James Casey shot him down in the street.

While all sorts of lies were being written about them and most outlandish accusations being made, the Community continued quietly about their business, establishing Mercy in this unruly place. Mother Baptist maintained a policy of serene silence which of course won the day. The hospital patients and former patients, many of whom were Protestants, refuted all the false claims made against the Sisters.

The city was in the grip of a self-appointed group of vigilantes who drilled on Stockton St. outside the hospital. The whole city was in terror of these people. A San Francisco housewife wrote the following extract about the activities of this unsavoury band:

"Many can neither eat nor sleep; they say the law and order people will plunder and burn the city and there is no knowing what will become of women and children. I assure you it looks very like war to go through our streets in the evening and see thousands of bayonets glimmering in the moonlight, going through their different evolutions, everyone showing grim determination to carry their point."

Mother Baptist was a regular visitor to the County Jail where James Casey had been taken after the shooting of King, followed by a mob yelling, "Kill him! Lynch Casey!" The Archbishop knowing that Casey would probably be the victim of popular fury requested permission to visit him, but was refused. Casey then asked for the help of the Sisters of Mercy to prepare him for his death. Mother Baptist with her usual courage in the face of grave personal danger wrote to the Committee of Vigilance for permission to visit the prisoner. They of course refused. Thankfully the Committee of Vigilance disbanded in August 1856.

Executions often took place in the County jail, an institution visited regularly by the Sisters.

Mother Baptist's interest in salvaging these lost souls is evident from the fearlessness which the Sisters showed when visiting these condemned men. They were sometimes locked in a cell with prisoners whom even the brutal guards feared. There is the story of the Sisters' part in the case of "Tipperary Bill" a particularly fierce character who was hanged in the yard of the Broadway jail on June 10th 1859.

"We visit the jail continually and find there many sad cases. We prepared two prisoners for execution; the last was hanged three weeks ago. He was a well-known robber, the terror of the country. He was called "Tipperary Bill", but his real name was William Morris. For many years the authorities had been endeavouring to capture him, but woe to the man who came near Bill; he would shoot him down and be off, no one knew where. At last came the time when Providence decreed he should be taken, and he was lodged in the County jail. He was not there long when he was detected cutting his chains. He was then heavily chained both hands and feet, and an immense thick chain around his ankle was attached to a ring in the ground. He was like a wild beast, and men were afraid to approach him.

When the Sisters went to visit him the jailer would not open the door unless he had two men with him, so great was the terror of Bill. They seemed astonished that we were not afraid of being admitted to so desperate a character. At first we thought him very hardened and so he was. It was very difficult to bring him to any idea of repentance until the trial was over and the death sentence passed. Even then, he said he would never give into the Yankees to laugh at him hanging in the air. The poor creature was terribly tempted to destroy himself, and for some time we did not dare to leave a holy water bottle with him for fear he might use the glass as a knife to cut his throat. During the trial Mother Gabriel's brother was near him in court; he described the prisoner as being a most ferocious looking man with the fire of anger and desperation flashing from his eyes.

Well, we visited him frequently, were locked in the cell with him, and though still savage to all others the poor fellow was gentle with us. On all the cell doors there is a little grating which is kept open during the day so visitors can speak through it to the prisoners. This was kept closed in the cell of William Morris so that he did not have a glimpse of light except from a candle. By conversing with him, we found that he had never received his First Communion and had been to Confession but once in his life. By constantly visiting him and giving him books to read, we succeeded under God in touching his heart. He made a general Confession, received his First Holy Communion and was confirmed by the good Archbishop who also invested him in the scapular.

He gave up talking to anyone but the Sisters and the priests. As the time of his execution came near we visited him every day and generally found him engaged in prayer. He was a very intelligent man, and other circumstances would have made him an ornament to society in appearance, manner and conduct. The poor fellow was greatly effected when we brought him holy water; he said he well remembered his mother sprinkling it around his bed.

When the morning of his execution came we were with him from nine until half-past eleven. Father brought him Holy Communion. He was so penitent and resigned that we were moved to tears, but they were tears of joy and gratitude to God for permitting us to be instruments in such a wonderful change. He thought we wept in pity at his untimely end and said, "Don't grieve; it's glad you ought to be that I die to-day. It's long years since I had the peace of mind that fills my heart this morning." On the scaffold his demeanour surprised everyone, and the change in "Tipperary Bill" was the subject of conversation among all classes and parties." (Letter from Sr.Francis Benson to the Sisters in Kinsale July 4th1859. Copy in the Burlingame Archives.)

Reports of the needs of prisoners in 1871 in the State Penitentiary - San Quentin - caused Mother Baptist to write to the Governor of the State requesting permission for the Sisters to visit these poor forgotten souls. There were strict rules barring all women visitors at that time, so she was delighted when she received the following reply from the Governor on April 11th 1871:

Sister Mary Baptist Russell

Dear Reverend Mother

The Sisters of Mercy may visit the State Prison at their convenience. It would probably be best to have regular times for visits, but you can confer as to this with the warden.

Respectfully yours

H.H.Haight (Governor of California)

So it came to pass that the Sisters visited San Quentin twice a month for the next forty years. Until 1893 Mother Russell herself led this work of Mercy, making it a point to visit Death Row. On two occasions she went to great lengths to obtain a pardon for prisoners, sparing their families back East the shame of knowing their loved ones died in prison. Both men were dying. She had one removed to St.Mary's hospital where he died peacefully in February 1893. The other man, whose pardon she had obtained in February 1872, died before the papers arrived, so she had his remains taken to the Mortuary Chapel at St.Mary's from where he was buried. She then wrote to his grieving mother.

The prisoners were so grateful for her untiring efforts on their behalf that they got permission and wrote an open letter in the local paper expressing their gratitude.

Editor of the Monitor

Dear Sir:

At the request of the Catholic prisoners confined here and by the kind permission of Captain J.C. Edgar, we beg leave to publicly express through your columns our heartfelt thanks to Mother Russell and the Sisters of Mercy under her charge at St.Mary's Hospital for the many and varied services rendered to the unfortunate inmates of this prison.

The influence of the Sisters upon the prisoners is next to that of a priest, and many a man has been made to see the light and find a cure for his despair in the kind words and Christian teaching of these good Sisters. Men in convict garb are still human beings, capable of reasoning, and susceptible to the influence of what is good. Many of them, through the Sisters' visits have been convinced of the errors of their career, and fortified by grace their complete reformation is made possible.

The work of the Sisters of Mercy at San Quentin does not stop there. It reaches into the homes and hearts of relatives and friends. Many a discharged prisoner has been given aid to enable him to lead an honourable life. The prisoners want, by this letter, to make known their appreciation of the untiring zeal of the Sisters of Mercy on their behalf. We wish too to thank them for the three hundred books they have brought to us during the last few years.

Sincerely yours on behalf of the prisoners,

J.J. Howard

T.J. Whelan.

People who knew Mother Baptist well all agree that her love of the poor was her most outstanding trait.

One of her Noviceship Companions, Sister Mary Elizabeth, made the following remarks:

"As for the poor, it used to be one of my greatest ambitions to be sent with her on visitation, especially to the Workhouse. You know the state of misery they were in there at the time, and it would touch any heart to see how tenderly she consoled them and helped them in their miseries. However calm she was under her own trials, I have seen her shed bitter tears on our way home from the Workhouse at the thought of the widespread wretchedness she had just witnessed and could do so little to relieve. Any little extra time or freedom she might have was always devoted to helping the poor in some way or other. She did many things in this way that

were not always approved of, but she did them with so much simplicity and good faith that no one could be annoyed. She was one of the most loving and generous souls I have ever met."

Mother Baptist made it her business to know those most in distress and to aid them to the very limit of her means. Her warm-hearted sympathy and practical service were valued more than the material help she gave. Making her way through the debris and mire of San Francisco's alleys, she would enter the miserable hovels of the poor, pin up her habit, put on an apron, scrub out the place, make up the bed of the sick with the fresh linen she had brought, wash the children, get a fire going, start a savoury stew and in a short time completely transform the atmosphere of the little home.

Archbishop Alemany once told Mother B. that her heart was bigger than her purse.

She was reputed to be a good listener and would listen for hours while poor unfortunates poured out their tales of woe.

She gained the friendship and respect of many of the Irish community who had made fortunes in the Golden State, people who were always ready to assist her worthwhile projects. They generously financed the building projects which she undertook.

During the 1870's she concentrated her attention on establishing educational facilities. She was responsible for founding some of the finest schools in the State of California where many fine citizens and future leaders received their education. One lady speaking of Mother Baptist says that as a schoolgirl she revered her as a saint and has not since changed her opinion. *"I never knew anybody who so closely portrayed the life of Our Lord. We loved to have her give our religious instructions, and for many years she reserved this duty for herself although she had innumerable important calls on her time. She told Bible stories in such a fascinating way and so earnestly that we were deeply impressed. The Scriptural quotations were so often repeated in appropriate places in the course of her instructions so that we learned them without any labour; in fact, her classes were the ones we most loved. Many of the early pupils of Our Lady of Mercy School became religious; I feel that they would unite with me in attesting that they owe their vocation, under God, to the beautiful Gospel lessons she impressed on our young minds. All loved her; she was gentle and kind to us, and always so interested in our sodalities and entertainments; she gave us great encouragement."* (San Francisco Post 1879)

During her forty-four years she developed a deep and abiding love for her adopted home. She loved to relax in the Californian landscape, whose history and mythology she studied. She collected many "treasures" during her walks in the hillsides, all of which she labelled. Some of these she donated to the Museum of Archaeology at the first Catholic University of America.

In 1891 Mother Baptist had suffered a slight stroke after which she resumed her normal activities. On July 4th 1898 she got up as usual, but when Mother Columba Kelly, her Assistant, saw how ill she looked she persuaded her to return to bed. This was the beginning of the end. During the next five weeks she steadily grew worse, and gradually her senses one after another became dulled by the clogging of the arteries to the brain.. Her family in Ireland was contacted and on August 6th 1898 she died. From the time of hearing of her illness the newspapers of the city gave daily reports of her condition. When she died there was full-page coverage paying tribute to her in every newspaper. Thousands of people visited the Chapel of the "Hospital on the Hill" to pay their last respects to one who had loved them so much. On the morning of her funeral the Chapel was packed two hours before the Requiem Mass, and the street outside was thronged with people. Archbishop Riordan celebrated the Mass and over fifty priests filled the sanctuary. Rev. Hugh Gallagher S.J., nephew of the Father Gallagher who brought Mother Russell to San Francisco, spoke lovingly about her life.

The Chronicle of the next day reported:

"No dead sovereign ever had prouder burial than Mother Mary Baptist whose life of self-denial and good works has crowned her in the city's memory. The great crowd literally besieged St.Mary's Hospital where her body was lying yesterday morning and swelled to such immense proportions when the graveyard was reached that the utmost efforts of a band of policemen were hardly sufficient to hold it in restraint."

In 1915 in a book entitled "The Makers of Northern California", among full page photographs and biographical sketches of about ninety men chosen for their contribution to the building of the state, there appears one woman- Mother Mary Baptist Russell - listed as "Pioneer Mother Superior in Northern California".

Mother Aquin Russell
Newry

Elizabeth Russell followed her sister Mother Baptist to St.Josephs, Kinsale. Before the completion of her Novitiate she returned to her native Newry as Assistant to Mother Catherine O'Connor when the Newry foudation was made in 1855. She has been described as having "sweet, tender, pitiful blue eyes".

She did not enjoy good health but she was always joyful and worked hard establishing Mercy in Newry where she made her profession on March 26th 1856. She served the Newry Community as Novice Mistress and Mother Assistant until she went as Superior to the branch house at Rostrevor in 1865.

She was a great writer of letters. Her many friends looked forward to receiving her warm and loving missives.

The severe pain, which she suffered in her last years was borne with brave resignation. Reading was her chief natural alleviator of the pain. Sadly she died on August 1st 1876. She was in her forties and was the first of the Russell sisters to die.

Sarah was the fourth child of Margaret and Arthur Russell. She was a pretty, sweet looking girl with large serious grey eyes and sunny golden brown hair. She was a fun loving girl who enjoyed keeping house. She loved baking and according to her brother Fr.Matthew Russell, made the most delicious cakes. Like all the Russell children she was well educated and well read.

Rev.Henry O'Neill, Bishop of Dromore, said that in Sarah Russell who became Sr.Emmanuel; "...the most amiable human qualities were blended with all the virtues that became a perfect religious -" praise indeed for the third Russell girl who was born on March 8th 1831. She worked as a catechist at the Newry Cathedral, preparing children for Confirmation and First Communion.

She walked two miles to Mass each morning. She wanted to be a nun and all that she did was in preparation for that. Being the youngest of the sisters she looked after her mother in her final years. She joined her sister at the Convent of Mercy, Newry, and threw herself into the works of Mercy with the same enthusiasm with which she had cared for her mother. She became Superior of the foundation in Lurgan where she earned the love and respect of all with whom she came in contact. With advancing years her sight failed. This must have been a huge trial, but she never grumbled, graciously accepting the assistance offered her by her beloved Community. She died on March 8th1902.

Mother De Sales Reddan
San Francisco

Joanna Reddan entered St.Joseph's, Kinsale, in 1849. It had been her wish for many years to become a Religious Sister, but the death of two of her sisters left her with six orphaned children to raise and educate so for forty years she gave up her own wishes.

Described as a noble motherly lady she became friends with Catherine McAuley, having met her in 1838 when she brought her niece, Joanna Bridgeman - yes, the famous Mother Francis - to her. At that time she confided her hopes and dreams to the foundress.

Joanna was born of wealthy respectable parents in Co.Clare close to the river Shannon. Hers was a happy home. At the age of seventeen she inherited a huge fortune. Limerick, then a garrison town, was where she decided to make her home. In 1819 she built a large stone house which became known as a Magdalen Asylum, a refuge for young women and girls where she taught needlework and the famous Limerick Lace. When cholera broke out in 1832 she nursed the victims, helped by many of her girls. Her eighteen-year-old niece, Joanna Bridgeman, "the belle of Limerick", took charge of the asylum while Joanna set to work among those stricken by the plague. The situation became so desperate that her niece, with the remaining Magdalen women, followed her aunt into the crowded hospitals.

When Catherine McAuley established the Sisters of Mercy in Limerick, the tall and sweet natured Miss Bridgeman joined them. Joanna Reddan also wanted to join the Sisters of Mercy and hand her Magdalen Asylum over to them, but her Bishop would not allow her. However in 1847 the Bishop allowed her to go to France and invite the Sisters of the Good Shepherd to take over her home. When these Sisters arrived, the Bishop ordered her to join them! "If you do not" he said, "I shall send them all back to France." She felt she had to comply with his command, but after a year in the Novitiate she knew that the Good Shepherd was not the Congregation to which she felt called. She withdrew and joined the Sisters of Mercy, following her beloved niece to Kinsale. At her reception she took as her patron St.Francis De Sales and was henceforth known as Sister De Sales. She was a distinguished highborn lady with a splendid fortune. She had all that this world held dear, just like her friend Catherine McAuley, yet she chose the simple life of a Sister. Her surname Reddan apparently comes from an ancestor called Dan who had red hair. She was reputedly related to Daniel O'Connell, the Liberator.

No doubt it was with great sadness that Mother Francis Bridgeman said good-bye to her aunt in 1854 when she formed part of the founding group bound for San Francisco. Sr.De Sales Reddan was chosen because of her experience and wisdom and as a mentor to the young Mother Baptist Russell.

Mother De Sales accompanied Mother Baptist to Sacramento to make arrangements for a new foundation. They had to travel by steamer and because they both suffered from seasickness they had to stay out on deck all night. Unfortunately they both caught colds. Mother De Sales did not recover and sadly died four days later in July 1857, just two years after their arrival in the city of St.Francis. In that short time she had so earned the love and respect of her adopted city that her death was mourned for quite some time. One man claimed that he would prefer to be scolded by Mother De Sales than praised by someone else! The little Community was devastated by the loss of this motherly figure so early in the mission. She had guided the young Superior thus far and would no doubt continue to do so from Heaven.

Mother Teresa Maher
Cincinnati

Anne Marie, daughter of Thomas and Maria Maher, was born in Carlow in 1824. She came from a family abounding in nuns and priests including two Cardinals! When Anne Marie was only thirteen years old the Sisters of Mercy came to Carlow. She probably went with her parents to a reception held for the Sisters at Carlow's Diocesan College. There she would have seen for the first time Catherine McAuley's friend and companion "Fanny" Warde - Mother Francis, Superior of the new Foundation.

Anne Marie was a bright girl who achieved at school, but her great love was music at which she excelled. In 1845, having completed her education and become a trained musician, she entered the Convent of Mercy, Kinsale, at the age of twenty-one. Taking the name Teresa at her reception, she made her first profession in 1847. Clearly she had qualities of leadership and was deeply spiritual as she was chosen first novice mistress to the fledgling Community. Previously Mother Francis had taken responsibility for the Religious Formation of the young girls who were joining them. When Mother Bridgeman went to the Crimea Mother Teresa was elected by the Community to succeed her as Superior. A contemporary of hers described her as "a religious of superior virtue and a woman of marked ability, integrity and beneficence, whose maturity of judgement and prudence of conduct outreached her years."

She was merely thirty years old when the persistent Mrs.Peter confronted her with the request for a foundation in Cincinnati. The prayers of the Community were offered for this venture and Mother Teresa liaised with Bishop Delaney and the Archbishop of Cincinnati in a most practical and competent way to ensure the security of the Sisters. Despatching Sisters to some unknown territory on the other side of the world called for responsible action on all sides. Here is a copy of the letter which Mother Teresa wrote to Archbishop Purcell:

My dear Lord,

You have heard, I presume, ere this of Mrs.Peter's visit to Kinsale and that we have promised (should nothing unforeseen occur) to send a foundation to Cincinnati, provided an adequate support can be secured for such a foundation. I beg to mention a few other conditions which I named to Mrs.Peter and which it may be well to state again for your Lordship's approval and sanction: that the Sisters be afforded the blessing of daily Mass in their Convent; that no duties be pressed on the Sisters which are not in accordance with the spirit of our holy Rule which states as the objects of our special duty "the service of the poor, sick and ignorant" under every circumstance, whether sick in a hospital, prisoners in a penitentiary, children in a school. We consider these to be our primary objects of care and devoted attention. We do not consider a boarding school at all in accordance with the word or spirit of our Rule; we should have no objection to aid in retreats, mentioned in your note, provided separate apartments could be arranged for ladies making these retreats.

Mrs.Peter gives us to understand that we need have no apprehensions regarding the means of support; that her income amounts to £800 per year, £200 per annum of which will be given during her life for the support of the Sisters; that on her return, it is her intention to insure her life, so that after her death, the Community may be secure (it being quite contrary to our Rule to labour for our support). Will you now, my Lord, guarantee that all these stipulations shall be adhered to and that should Mrs.Peter be called out of this life before the insurance should be available, our Sisters shall not want the necessaries of life. We, (our good Bishop included), consider such a guarantee from your Lordship's hand indispensable before undertaking such a mission at such a distance. We have never sent out, nor should we think it prudent to send out, Sisters on such a mission without having had previously a promise of protection, patronage and co-operation from the Bishop of whatever diocese they were going to. We consider the Diocesan Bishop in spirituals and temporals our parent and guardian. As preparations are suspended by our Bishop till we receive a reply to this, may I beg your Lordship's earliest attention to its purport."

The Archbishop agreed to all the conditions (even though at a later date he failed them), and the Sisters set off on Friday July 23rd 1858. Mother Teresa was of course the leader of the group, assisted by Mother Gertrude O'Dwyer. Bishop Delaney was loathe to part with any of the Sisters, but especially Mother Teresa whom he hoped would return to Kinsale when the foundation was established.

The early years of the foundation were fraught with difficulties. Several young Sisters died, and the financial problems placed a great strain on Mother Teresa and her Sisters. They engaged in all sorts of fund-raising activities to defray their expenses. Of course the lack of personnel to work in the various Mercy initiatives added to the stress.

Mother Teresa's term of leadership came to an end in 1864 when she would have gladly handed the reins to another. However the Community lacked the minimum number of professed Sisters for a canonical election. Archbishop Purcell insisted that Mother Teresa be returned to office. The question arose again three years later in 1867, and yet again Mother Teresa's wish to resign office was thwarted because the Community unanimously elected her Superior.

By 1875 Mother Teresa's health was failing rapidly. She confided to her friend Mother Austin Carroll, author of "Leaves of the Annals of the Sisters of Mercy":

"I have been in poor health since July. My dearest friend, God has sent me a salutary warning to remind me to keep my lamp always trimmed and replenished, in the shape of heart disease. This has snatched my mother, two brothers and a sister. Pray that I may not go suddenly. Your letters and prayers have been a great support to me during our trials. I bless God you prosper so well in the South and I trust the roots will grow deep as the branches extend. I write with great difficulty. Sometimes I cannot write at all. Always remember me in your pious prayers, my dearly beloved friend."

Ill as she was she continued to lead the Community, and, being the musician she accompanied all the Masses and hymns, "not only with religious feeling but with educated taste as well", according to her biographer, Sister Margaret Moliter RSM.

The Community Obituary Book describes her accompaniment to the 1875 Christmas Mass *"...And Mother got along nicely until the end of the Gloria. As the Gloria was intoned she played with all the vigour of her soul and with such expression that one could feel that she was very near God. At the last chord Mother stopped instantly and had to be removed from the organ bench for she was unable to move. However restoratives were administered and she revived, but it was the beginning of the illness that took her before another Christmas...."*

July 1876 saw her again being elected to the office of Mother Superior. Shortly afterwards, feeling unequal to the duty she wrote to Archbishop Purcell for permission to retire. He refused her request. By the end of October she was again very weak and unable to get up. When Archbishop Purcell visited her she begged him to allow her to resign her office, but he again refused. On the feast of St.Cecilia - Patron of Music- November 22nd she died. She was just fifty-three years old.

Her Requiem Mass was celebrated by the Archbishop who was several times overcome by grief. Most of the clergy and people of Cincinnati attended her funeral. "The Catholic Telegraph" for November 27th 1876 paid the following tribute to Mother Teresa Maher:

"None will lament the loss of Mother M.Teresa more than the poor and suffering of this city to whom she was a ministering Angel. In prison and hospital, in garret and cellar, wherever the needy and suffering are to be found, Mother Teresa was a familiar presence."

The Cincinnati Annalist writes:

"Mother Teresa was undoubtedly one of the great women of the Order, and her works remain to praise her in the gate. Her children rise up to call her blessed. She was not handsome in the face but had a sweet, intelligent expression, and uncommon intellectual endowments. As an organist she ranked among the best in the country. Her most salient characteristic was uprightness, and she was in every relation of life the soul of honour and sincerity. She had the name of being severe, and she certainly had nothing in her composition of the softness that leads to self-indulgence or passes over as trifling, delinquencies that may have serious consequences. But no one made larger allowances for human frailty; often she said of her children: "They are doing the best they can; they mean well; we shall all be perfect when we go to heaven." Large hearted, generous and trusting, she combined the simplicity of a child with mature wisdom. She loved the young with special tenderness, and her relations with them were marked with a genial warmth."

Mother Teresa's sister Mother Philomena Maher was part of the foundation to Clonakilty. In 1860 she led the foundation to Skibbereen, but returned to Kinsale in her later years. She is buried in the convent cemetery Kinsale.

The Women of Ireland

Mná na hEireann so often praised by Ireland's former President, Mrs. Mary Robinson, certainly had authentic and boundary stretching role models in these remarkable women, - women I feel whose praises have not been sung or honoured in the corridors of power. They actually lived by the phrase "Care in the Community" long before it was coined in the twentieth century. May we never forget the debt of gratitude we owe these brave women who sailed into the uncharted waters of health care, education and social work long before the National Health System, the Social Services and the Education System were even thought of.

Chapter 4
The Three Marys
Kinsale's Three Centenarians

Is it too much of a coincidence that these three ladies were called Mary and each one was born in September?

They lived through many changes: - through two world wars, the troubled era of our own history, the 1916 rising, the founding of the state and the heartbreak of the civil war. They saw the most appalling poverty and deprivation as well as the increased affluence of the eighties and nineties. They were part of the huge changes in Religious life in the wake of Vatican 11. They remembered the nine popes of the twentieth century. They saw men walk on the moon!

Mary O'Grady (Sister Imelda)

Mary O'Grady was born in Ballinacurra, Co.Limerick, on September 6th 1890. Her parents, Stephen and Mary O'Grady, had five children, two boys and three girls. The young Mary attended primary school in Limerick City, and when she was of age to go to secondary school, she went as a boarder toConvent of Mercy, Doon. Doon of course had been founded from Kinsale in 1865.

Mary first visited Kinsale in 1895, when she was four years old to see her great aunt, Sr.M.Raphael Sexton, who was close to death at the time. I doubt if she then thought that this Convent would become her home thirteen years later! On September 24th, Mercy Day, in 1908 she entered St.Joseph's. On April 26th 1911 she made her first profession.

When she came to Kinsale the town was dominated by military, coastguard and RIC personnel, the local economy was heavily dependent on these. The fishing industry was in decline so there was widespread poverty.

She trained as a Primary School teacher, Teacher training in those days was done through inservice training, backed up by courses usually taken during the school holidays. So she taught in the Primary School until after retirement, when she taught Religious Education to the girls in the Secondary School.

Sister Imelda was an excellent communicator and loved people, especially young people she devoted her whole life to them having worked in both schools. She looked after firstly: - the orphans many of whom wrote to her until the time of her death, and later the boarders who also remember her with great affection. A warm woman with motherly qualities, she made the transition from home to boarding school less painful for the children than it might have been.

Mother Imelda kept the convent annals for many years, and they are a delight to read. She recorded the day to day events of the community in a coherent and interesting way. Being a well-read, well-informed woman who could speak about anything, she was also very entertaining, an altogether gracious lady.

In September 1990 she celebrated her hundredth birthday. An event she wished to keep secret but one of her relatives telephoned Gay Byrne's Radio shows, and the "cat was out of the bag". Chairman of the Town Council Mr Dermot Ryan, presented her with a plaque of the town's coat of arms on behalf of the people of Kinsale. Greetings and tributes poured into the Convent from former orphanage children, from as far afield as U.S.A. South Africa, Ghana, Pakistan and Hong Kong, people with whom she had kept up a correspondence over the years and from family and friends far and wide.

In her latter years she still felt she had a mission to spend her days praying for all those who had touched her life, the needs of the Church and the world.

Sr.Imelda became Mother Assistant of the Community in 1936 and went on to become superior in 1942. Until the 1970s she was either Rev.Mother or Mother Assistant, duties she dispensed with kindness and understanding.

She died at the wonderful age of 105 in May 1995.

Mary Lynch (Sister Emmanuel)

Mary, daughter of John and Margaret Lynch of Ballybunion Co.Kerry was born on September 13th1891. She was one of a very large family, many of whom emigrated to various parts of the globe.

She entered the convent in Kinsale on October 8th1910, where she made her first profession on May 5th1914.

During her early days in Kinsale Sister Emmanuel taught in the infant school, I am sure some of the older people in the town still remember her, of course her cousin Sister Mary Rose, taught many generations of Infants in Kinsale.

After her short sojourn in the infant school Sr.Emmanuel became a nurse. She was the first Sister to be sent for advanced training to the Mercy Hospital in Cork. Previously doctors and senior nurses trained nurses, while they were actually doing the job.

She worked at the old hospital in Friars Street with Mother Antonia who was matron there. Together with Mother Antonia she was responsible for the moving of patients to the present hospital, which of course was the old workhouse. She often recalled the hardship of that old hospital in Friar St.

Sr.Emmanuel was hospital matron until her retirement in 1956. She brought her common sense and practical skills to the setting up of this hospital and driven by a sense of service and devotion she worked hard for the sick of the town. A kind and generous friend to the poor, a humble woman who did not "blow her own trumpet". She earned the respect of all with whom she worked. Walking had been one of her delights; she would often embark on a really long hike, exhausting her much younger companions! In fact having suffered much from her feet and legs, she continued exercising until she was nearly 100.

After her retirement she took on the role of bursar at the convent, a post she held until the nineteen seventies. In this role she meticulously managed the finances of the community.

Sister Emmanuel was always active; well into her old age she supplied soft toys, which she made for all sorts of fundraising events in the schools, the parish and in the town generally. In fact she became quite famous for her craftwork, which contributed hundreds of pounds to charity.

During her long life she visited Ballybunion annually, firstly for day-trips with a companion, then for her two nights after 1967, and later for longer periods until 1992 when she was no longer able to travel. She retained a very special love for her native Kerry

She celebrated her hundredth birthday in 1991, when family came from all over Ireland, from the U.S.A. and from Australia to be with her. Her sister, a Poor Clare nun aged eighty-eight, flew in from Sidney. Her nephew, Fr.Charles O'Connor, a Jesuit, was Chief Celebrant at the Concelebrated Mass. It was a wonderful occasion for her and for the whole community. Her ambition at this time was to visit the hospital and have a "spin" in the new lift, which had been recently installed there.

She died on September 18th 1994 aged 103, in the hospital where she had served for so long.

Mary Sheehan (Sister Fachtnan)

Sister Mary Fachtnan has the rare distinction of having lived in three centuries, and was awarded a special medallion by our President Mary McAleese to honour this extraordinary achievement.

Born Mary Sheehan on September 5th 1898 on the beautiful island of Cape Clear, off the West Cork coast, she jokingly considered herself a foreigner. She also boasted that "the faith" was alive and well on Cape Clear before the arrival of St.Patrick, thanks to St.Ciaran. Mary's parents, Thomas and Julia Sheehan, had seven children, five of whom survived. One of her brothers served in the Royal Navy in both world wars and lived to the grand old age of ninety-one as did another brother Thade. We know that one of her sisters, Julia, emigrated to England and became a nurse. Unfortunately she died of T.B. when she was only forty-four years of age.

Mary's father was a fisherman working in "Roaring Water Bay" in his boat "The Sagart".

As a young girl Mary used to sail on this boat with her Dad and brothers and sisters. It sounds a very idyllic way of life to us today, but in many ways it was a hard and dangerous life, living always at the mercy of the elements. On one occasion she took a boat out alone as far as the Fastnet, much to the consternation of her family as she was quite young at the time.

Mary loved her island home, from there she brought her gentle and loving disposition, her great wisdom and her absolute trust in God, and like our Celtic ancestors a prayer for every occasion. She also brought the special lace making and crotchet skills peculiar to Cape Clear, and much of her beautiful work can be seen on the Altar at Kinsale and in the Museum on her native Cape Clear.

She entered the Convent of Mercy, Kinsale, on July 8th 1919. She must have found it very strange and confining, after the freedom of life in such close proximity to nature on her island home.

On January 22nd 1922 she made her profession. She did not see Cape Clear again until 1933, when she made her 1st day trip home, accompanied by the late Sr. Cecilia O'Flynn, driven to

Baltimore in a car owned by the late Mylie Murphy. This was the pattern of her annual visit until 1967 when the sisters got permission to stay two nights per year in their own homes. Imagine her delight spending two nights back on Oileán Chléire. She has seen many, many changes. When it became possible for the sisters to travel, Sr. Fachtnan took the opportunity to visit Knock, Lourdes and Fatima, as well as visiting her niece, Sr.Therese, in London.

She brought great culinary skills from her home, and spent many years in charge of catering for the orphans for whom she had a special love, for the boarders most of whom remember her with great affection, and of course for her beloved community.

She has a great interest in people, and was a trusted friend to many.

She has never lost her interest in the Irish Language and folklore. At one hundred and three years young she still speaks the "Gaeilge" fluently. She is able to get up every day, in the Nursing Home for elderly sisters in Tralee, where she is so well cared for.

May we continue to be blest by her gentle presence and encouraged by the example of her prayerful life.

Sr. Fachtnan died on October 23rd 2001. May she Rest In Peace.

CONVENT OF MERCY, KINSALE 1994

Pat Lordan - Past Pupil of Our Lady of th Rosary School

Chapter 5
St. Joseph's in the 20th Century

Sister Joseph Keohane entered the Convent of Mercy Kinsale on April 1st. 1938. She spent many years nursing in the Hospital succeeding Sr.Emmanuel Lynch as matron, a post she held until 1985. She recalls her early years in Kinsale.

"If I could transport myself back to the town of Kinsale of 1946, I would find it vastly different from the prosperous town it is today. At that time there was poverty, unemployment, malnutrition and illness. These were the facts of life for most people, and last but not least the housing was poor.

I commenced my nursing career in the Cottage Hospital as it was then known. This was the time of the Economic War when everything was scarce - food, medicines, hospital supplies and fuel - and to add to that problem every bed and cot in the hospital was occupied. The maternity unit and nursery were flourishing, but there was a great shortage of midwives. Sister Emmanuel, the matron at that time, decided I should do my maternity training. There was a great deal of Red Tape in the process of getting permission, first from the Rev.Mother, and then from the Bishop, because "it was never done before!" Eventually the permission came through but I couldn't stay in the training school accommodation at the Erinville - I had to stay in a Convent. The Convent I stayed in was in Sunday's Well and that was one mile from the Erinville, therefore it meant I walked to and from work six days a week, - we had one day off. Thank God through many tribulations I completed my course after twelve months, and was overjoyed coming back to Kinsale.

It didn't take me long to get into the full swing of work in the hospital and to quote a Kinsale saying "I borned" many a baby from then on, and thank God there was never a casualty. Sadly today they do not have a maternity unit in Kinsale as in any of the District Hospitals – too much Red Tape again, and also there isn't an obstetrician on the staff.

In 1957 the then Matron Sr. Emmanuel retired and I was appointed to her post. I kept in mind a saying from a wise senior sister – "Make haste slowly", so I got my bearings, and left everything as it was until the staff got acquainted with my style of doing things. I was much younger than some of the staff. As the economy was improving and there was a little more money in circulation, I realised that the hospital should be modernised somehow. Another point in my favour, the then Health Board was in favour of upgrading the District Hospitals. They set about converting storerooms, which were not in use into wards, and that meant we had a modern thirteen-bed unit, which was opened as an orthopaedic unit. Male and Female post-operative patients were transferred from Cork four or five days after operation, and these patients remained in Kinsale until the visiting orthopaedic surgeon was satisfied that they were fit for home. The physiotherapist on the staff was a great help in mobilising all the patients. The physiotherapy unit was a very busy place both for in-patients and out-patients.

To mention some more improvements, a new fire-alarm system was installed throughout the hospital, also a new mortuary and post- mortem room. The latter was a great facility because prior to that a doctor had to come from Cork city to do a post-mortem in very low grade facilities. At this time a great "stroke of luck" came our way, the Management of an American factory in Kinsale offered to help in any way to improve conditions in the hospital. They installed weather- glaze windows throughout the hospital and these were invaluable for preserving heat. At a later stage they erected railings and curtains around the beds in each of the wards – that surely was a bonus. All these improvements were a great asset for the running of the hospital.

I must pay tribute to the excellent staff, both nursing and domestic, who co-operated in so many ways in the successful running of the hospital. This was something I could not have done on my own - teamwork was of the greatest importance.

But all good things must come to an end and it was with much sadness I finished my time in office on the 31stMarch 1985 I hope and pray that my years of service were an essential means of reaching out to the many needs of people wherever there was need.

I look with gratitude to the past, and with hope to the future knowing that "He who is mighty can do great things for us."

"The Industrial School quietly came to an end," says the Annals entry for September 1963. It had been founded in 1869 – the first of its kind in Ireland - and was certified for one hundred and eighty orphans or destitute children. Many of the former orphans emigrated to America and England and did well there. Quite a few entered Convents in America, England and South Africa. Some stayed in Ireland, married and raised families to be proud of. All to whom I have spoken remember the convent and the Sisters with great love and affection and like me consider it their home. Many still visit regularly, but sadly many of the Sisters whom they knew and loved have gone to their reward – Sister Dympna, Sister de Pazzi, Sister Assumpta (Maureen Ryan) and Sister Lawrence.

Sister Carmel Collins and Sister Yvonne Collins are past pupils of the school, though not related. On hearing of the closure of the Convent they sent the following letter to Sr.Immaculata Hourihane.

Augustinian Convent
P.O.Box 32
Estcourt 3310
Kura Zulu Natal

April 17th. 2001

Dear Kinsale Sisters living and now with God,

In response to an invitation to write an article for the Kinsale Convent Book I'm taking this opportunity to thank you all for having been God's gracious gift in my life and indeed in the lives of so very many other past pupils who have been through your hands. I speak now especially on behalf of Sr.Yvonne Collins and myself, as we are both in South Africa, serving God as Augustinian Sisters of the Mercy of Jesus.

Those of you who are now happy with God are still looking on us with loving interest. You touched us with love and led us to God, not only by what you taught us but also by praying with us and we know you are now praying for us. Only He knows how your influence has spread throughout the world by the very many vocations to the Religious Life which you inspired and fostered, as well as the good mothers of families, which you have formed. Each one of us was precious to you and we are now your flowers scattered in God's garden throughout the world. Your prayers also lovingly embrace those who have died, like Teresa Barry in Kinsale.

As for the future of the Convent building and grounds I'm sure you would wish them used, at least in part, for the benefit of God's work. Since Kinsale is so prosperous now and does not need the Convent, as in the days when life was much harder for us all, it still needs your presence there. We are not on the spot to take part in discussions with regard to the use of the buildings, but we will be praying for God's guidance for all concerned. I know that all will agree that the hallowed memory of your lives must be kept alive for future generations. We would wish them also to benefit from your legacy to us – one of grace, goodness, holiness and love.

Your ever-grateful pupils
Sr.M Carmel
Sr.M Yvonne

The Boarding School and Our Lady of the Rosary School opened in 1951. The Boarding School closed in 1984 and Our Lady of the Rosary School closed in 1996 when the Kinsale Community School opened. The new school cost £2.5 million has 520 students on roll and a staff of 35 teachers. The sole surviving Sister of Mercy in the School is Sr.Mary O'Donovan who is Principal.

Sister Mary O Donovan came to Kinsale from Skibbereen in August 1984 to teach science, mathematics, and religion for a term.

She returned in 1985 as Principal to the Convent Secondary School. She recalls how the new school came about.

"The congregation at Diocesan wished that and work should commence immediately to provide a new modern 2nd level school to cater for all the students in the Kinsale area.

Sr. Immaculata Murphy – Mother General and I started discussions with the Dept. of Education, staff and parents. All agreed on the need for a new school and following many meetings and information sessions the Dept. of Education sanctioned a new Community School in May 1988. However due to financial difficulties at National level the allocation of finance for school building at all levels was drastically reduced.

I worked closely with parents, lobbying for the school and together we made it a political issue, especially at election times. The lobbying consisted of meeting local politicians at their clinics regularly, going to Leinster House on two occasions and finally I organised and chaired two public meetings to which all public representatives (T.D.s, County Councillors and urban councillors, linked in any way to the school catchment area were invited.

The need for the school was obvious and the increased public pressure at the second open meeting produced results. Finance was allocated and work commenced on the school in January 1995. The main building was completed for September 1996. However due to increased enrolment an extension was sanctioned immediately and was completed for the official opening of the School on April 19th. 1999 – exactly 155 years after the Sisters of Mercy first came to Kinsale.

At that time the local contribution of 5% - £130,000 from the congregation or the local community, should be made to the Dept. of Education. The local community expected our new school to be a valuable resource and was very happy to get involved in fundraising. I organised fund-raising using the "planned giving" method over a twelve month period. Tremendous organisation and teamwork went into the fundraising. We were all extremely pleased and relieved when we achieved our goal.

Keeping in mind the smooth amalgamation of Our Lady of the Rosary School and the

Vocational School, the good working relationship I had with the two schools and the local community, I decided to apply for the post of Principal to facilitate the amalgamation. I was appointed to the post in April 1996. The amalgamation went very well bringing together the best of the two traditions.

The Community School provides a full range of subjects and caters for the needs of all 2nd. Level students, an adult day course in Business Studies and a wide range of evening classes."

During the Marian Year of 1954 an American priest came asking for Sisters to work in the diocese of St.Augustine in Florida. Those selected for this mission were Sisters Albert, Baptist, Teresita and Peter. They set off in August 1955.

Again in 1956 Fr.Kelligan the Pastor of Delray Beach, visited begging for more Sisters to work in Florida. Several volunteered but Sisters Bernard and Assumpta (Maureen Ryan) were chosen to go.

The late Sr. Maureen Ryan (Assumpta)

1958 saw the election of Pope John XX111, an elderly and loveable gentleman whose charisma charmed the world. In his short reign – he died in 1963 – he initiated changes that had far reaching effects. He aimed to make the Church relevant to the twentieth century. He summoned the cardinals and bishops to Rome for the Second Vatican Council, which opened in October 1962 and went on for two years after his death, closing on December 8th1965.

Sister Dolores Quill left for Delray Beach, Florida, in April 1962. Sister Bernadette Hurley followed suit in September 1963. Both Sisters had entered for that foundation. For some reason the Bishop then decreed that the practice of Sisters entering for a particular mission was to cease.

Another Convent institution was in decline by 1963. The Lace Room, which once employed one hundred and fifty workers, was now reduced to three women – Katty O'Regan, Julia Walsh and Nellie Holland. Kinsale lace was worn and appreciated by ladies, including royalty, all over the world - even Queen Victoria was given some.

Post Vatican Two – A time of huge Change.

The vernacular was introduced into the Mass, adaptations were being made to the Sister's dress. The coif, (a large circular piece of dress worn around the neck, and particularly stifling on a hot day!) was discarded in favour of the more manageable dimity. The Cork mission in Peru was launched, several priests and Sisters from the diocese were chosen to go. Our previous bishop Dr.Michael Murphy was in the first wave of priests to go. Sisters from Bantry and St.Maries of the Isle were the first group of Sisters to go. Sister Benignus Cremins, who spent many years working in the hospital in Kinsale and now looks after the elderly in the Sheltered Accommodation complex went to work in Peru in October 1971. Here she remembers her time in the hospital:

"On completion of my General and midwifery training I was appointed staff nurse in Kinsale District Hospital. Due to shortage of accommodation in the hospital I traveled to and from the Convent on foot, as cars were not easily available at that time. Eventually I secured a permanent post with accommodation in the hospital, which made life easier. I worked on male, female and midwifery wards, the maternity being my favourite place of duty. I now meet adults whom I delivered during that time. On Sister Joseph Keohane's retirement I was appointed matron, very much against my will.

Having accepted the appointment and having received a substantial donation from the family of a patient, I made an assessment of the needs of the hospital. A fundraising committee was formed and a lift installed. An Ensuite Room overlooking the garden for respite care and the terminally ill was opened. A sunlounge and a prayer room were provided.

Beds were made available for patients requiring nursing and long-term care on the ground floor.

I retired in October 1998 and Maureen O'Donovan was appointed matron. She now carries on the work the Sisters started in 1893.

I take this opportunity to thank the Sisters who worked and shared their lives with me, also the hospital staff who were always so helpful and accommodating. A special word of thanks to the Life Committee without whose help the improvements could not be possible".

Between 1964 and 1965 six postulants entered the Convent, this marked the last of the big numbers to enter. On the Feast of Christ the King, Halloween, the beginning of the Celtic New Year – Samhain October 31st, three postulants entered in Kinsale, Aileen Aherne, Kathleen Costin and myself. I mention this because Kathleen Costin who came from Waterford died two weeks later and is buried in the cemetery at the Convent. She was a dear soul. I thought she was really old, at twenty-seven! Her health was not good, but it had always been her wish to become a Sister of Mercy. Her family, though heartbroken, was delighted that she had got her wish. They visit her grave annually, and were always pleased to see her companions of only two weeks. Sr.Mary O' Donoghue joined the Kinsale community in June 1965. She remembers the postulant, her companion of just two weeks.

"The closing of Kinsale Convent evokes in me many memories of my years in that hallowed place. Having joined the Mercy Sisters in Kinsale in 1965 I lived there for twenty years. As I reflect back over the years, I recall many wonderful memories of people and events, in fact too many for the purpose of this book.

Aware that memories are being shared by a number of people I would like to recall one of my earliest – the memory of Kathleen Costin. I was four months in the Convent when Kathleen Costin, a native of County Waterford, along with Aileen Aherne and Joan O'Mahony joined me. My experience of Kathleen was of a gentle, kind and quiet person. The people of Kinsale did not know her, because her stay with us was short. Two weeks after her arrival, Kathleen became ill. Doctor O'Keeffe was called and arranged for her to be sent to the Mercy Hospital in Cork. Our novice mistress Sr.Oliver, asked me to pack Kathleen's case as she would not be returning to the Convent following her stay in hospital. Kathleen would have been disappointed with the decision as she had a real desire for Religious life. About fifteen minutes before the ambulance was due to arrive, while I was packing the case, news filtered through the Convent that Kathleen had died. This was a shock for all of us. Kathleen's family was contacted and they arrived later that evening. Her funeral Mass took place in our own chapel and Kathleen was buried in the Convent cemetery. Had she died in the ambulance or in hospital her funeral would have been elsewhere. Kathleen's desire was fulfilled. Kathleen's stay was short but her story left a deep impression on me.

Ar dheis Dé go raibh a hanam dílis."

Free education was introduced into Ireland in 1967. This greatly increased the numbers attending Our Lady of the Rosary Secondary School.

A branch house at Port Charlotte, Florida, was founded from Delray Beach in 1967 Sisters Assumpta (Maureen Ryan), Dolores and Bernadette were the founding Sisters there, and they were joined by Sr.Monica Aherne from Kinsale. In 1976 the Community in Kinsale voted to close this foundation.

Mary Aherne Thompson, formerly Sister Monica, who lives in the U.S.A. has very pleasant memories of her life as a Sister of Mercy:

"Mother Oliver had a great influence on my life. I learned a lot through her kindness, gentleness and understanding, and those qualities of hers helped me in my daily dealings with others.

I have great respect for the sisters past and present. Instead of being hurt by my decision to "abandon" them they have always welcomed me back to visit them with true sincerity and joy. I do hope that the transition from the old home to their new one will be as painless as possible. It saddens me to think that all those memories of good times and hard will be erased when the door closes for the last time."

Boys were admitted to the Secondary School in 1968. Over twenty male students, mostly first years, one Leaving Cert. Donal Goggin, three fifth years: Michael Buckley, Gerard Tierney and Michael Doran plus a few Inter Cert. Boys turned up on September 4th of that year.

In December 1968 the annals record that at a Junior Chamber of Commerce Talent Contest and Quiz held at Farranferris, Kinsale won the quiz and Pat Crowley excelled himself on the piano accordion and won the talent competition.

Pat, Kinsale's own "Mr Music", was in the first wave of boys to come to the school

He has brought great pride and honour to his school, his family and the wider Kinsale community, for the way in which he has used and honoured his great musical talent. As well as playing the backing music for Mary Black, he is a composer and recorded artist in his own right.

His memories here are of an earlier time when he attended the Convent Infant School.

"My first memory of the building would be of the Infant School, the big slightly bowed-from-use limestone step up into a tall narrow corridor leading to a lobby for the classroom's cloakroom and playground. The cloakroom didn't have a window – a single lightbulb hung there – too small for the job. In the mornings it would be full of kids jumping with their coats in hand trying to hook them on the coat hangers, and on a wet day the smell from the damp coats I will never forget.

The classroom was bright. It had two long Georgian type windows, which faced the playground. Sister Rose was our teacher, and even on a dull day outside she managed by her nature to brighten the room. She was a tall slim woman with a soft gentle face and she had a beautiful smile – the perfect first teacher experience.

For me the best part of her class was when we would play music in her percussion band. It comprised of tambourines, triangles and hand cymbals. Sr Rose would play the old walnut yellow-keyed grand piano that sat in the corner of the room, and we would all sing and play. The noise was wonderful, and it was my first band.

After two years we all moved down the corridor to what we called the sixes and sevens. The woman in charge was Sr.Raphael, a smallish woman who wore dispensary type glasses. It was

here that we prepared for First Confession and First Communion. She had more discipline than Sr.Rose and of her class I also have fond memories. She would have us marching around the classroom singing Old Irish marches, and at the end of the class there was what we called "The Shop". It comprised lots of different things, which the kids would bring into school, acorns, flowers, stones, dead birds, etc.

Sr.Raphael seemed to be always dealing with keys- large door keys, she must have been in charge of opening and closing the school. One rule she constantly quoted to us was; not to pass a certain point, which was known as the studio. From that point on it was the Secondary School.

From the convent the boys and girls separated after Infant School, the boys going on to the "Monks", as we called St.John's School which was run by the Presentation Brothers, and the girls to St Joseph's which was housed upstairs over the Secondary School in the Convent.

I remember when I was in sixth class Primary there was a lot of talk amongst us as to where we would be going to Secondary School. Hamilton High, Bandon was a favourite of Kinsale boys. Presentation College, Cork and Turners Cross were others.

Free Education was coming in around that time – 1968 - and there was talk of the Convent providing Secondary Education for boys.

This came to pass, and so I was part of the group that made up the first boys to attend Our Lady of the Rosary Secondary School."

1968 was a red-letter year for the Sisters as they were allowed to have £5 pocket money per year!

In that same year, Sister M.Clare Fennell was chosen to go to Delray Beach, where she still ministers at St.Vincent Ferrer's School. She has fond memories of her time in Kinsale.

"My time in Kinsale, prior to Florida, was spent in the Noviceship and Mary Immaculate Training College, Limerick.

Looking back on it now, those days were full of fun, laughter and experiencing community life in the midst of youth and frolic in the noviceship. I appreciated the simple things like our day trips to the beach driven by Fr.Willie Aherne R.I.P. We all enjoyed nature and our walks to the hills. I enjoyed the apples!

When I came to Florida I never experienced anything like the heat and no air-conditioning in the school or in the Convent. I taught second grade and loved the students. I did miss Ireland, my noviceship friends and my family.

At that time in America there was a great exodus from Religious life and the priesthood. I am *sure it made me stop and evaluate my own spirituality. I encountered divorce for the first time, and my heart ached for those students when they were so broken because Daddy or Mummy had left.*

Mother McAuley would be with the marginalised today. There is a great deal of loneliness and emptiness among our youth and senior citizens. Catherine would love them and help them appreciate who they are and try to model to them that God is madly in love with them. Our young people are depressed and get involved in drugs, drink or sex and this leads to suicide.

I believe the greatest pioneers were Mother Baptist Russell, who went to San Francisco from Kinsale at a very young age, Srs.Clare and Francis both worked in the Crimean War.

Our need in our local community is to empower lay people to take over and to let go and let God work. We can witness so much as our life is counter culture."

1968 was also the year that the Community got their first car – a gift from their American benefactress, Mrs Wetmore. Several members of the Community had driving lessons and took off to Skibbereen on Sunday afternoons with Mr. Thomas O'Donoghue (Sister Mary's father) who gave his time so generously to teach the Sisters to drive. It was possible in those days to take the driving test in Skibbereen, which of course was a much quieter route than the Cork City one.

It was a year of many gifts. I am not sure which caused the most excitement. High on the list was the two nights' "holiday" in their own homes, which of course meant three days and how the most benefit could be gained? – Some Sisters were setting off at dawn and returning on the stroke of nine so as to get as much time as possible with their loved ones!

The "real" Taoiseach, the late Jack Lynch accompanied by his wife Maureen visited the community on July 7th. They spent quite a long time in the Community Room chatting to individual sisters. Sister Raphael, as I recall, was radiant with delight.

The year of the Moonlanding, 1969 saw the two nights at home being extended to a week, a cause of great delight to young and old alike. Sr.Eleanor O'Leary recalls how this extension came about.

Sr. Raphael O'Sullivan

"The decision at Federation level was much debated. There were three of us from the various houses under thirty, with the remaining eighteen mostly comprising of Rev.Mothers and Mother Assistants. That is not to say that the latter group did not comprise of forward thinking people, such as Sr.Brigid Flanagan of Rosscarbery. I remember at the conclusion of the morning proceedings, the decision was not to extend the two nights at home. However when we

returned after lunch, the Mother President, Sr.Columba, said `Sr.Anthony if you are so upset about the decision, we could write to the Bishop, ` To which I replied `Yes, do. ` In my youthful ignorance, I thought that the Bishop might summon me to his presence subsequently! Instead a letter arrived which stated that the Bishop would be happy if the Sisters were to go home for a week since it was from these very homes vocations to Religious Life had been developed. The event taught me much about Religious women taking control of their own lives and not projecting lack of development onto Bishops!"

It was also a sad year for the Community as Sister Agatha Gurhy, a young sister who looked after the girls in the boarding school and who was much loved by all who knew her, died of cancer. It was a mark of her generous spirit, that she offered her pain for the examination success of the novices attending university.

Of course it was the year which marked the start of the present troubles in Northern Ireland. Prayers were said daily in Community for a solution to this impossible situation. We can only hope that after all this time we are now further along the road towards peace.

In 1972 Sr.M.Baptist returned from Florida as Superior, to be replaced by Sister Finbarr Morrissey.

The Convent played host to a party of refugees from Northern Ireland who were housed in the Boarding School. This "holiday" for the children, away from the violence, was arranged by the Civil Defence.

The Sisters voted for the first time in the 1973 General Election. It is difficult to believe that these women had been disenfranchised for so long. The right to vote was hard won by other courageous women.

Sisters Imelda, Cecilia, Fachanan, Ann and Carmel had their first air journey in 1974 when they went on a pilgrimage to Lourdes. This marked the beginning of four or five Sisters going to Lourdes each year.

The foundation stone was laid for the new Primary School in December 1976. The official opening ceremony was held in April 1978. Sister Mary McAuliffe was the very popular Principal of the Primary School who oversaw the smooth transition from the old school to the lovely new building on the Convent grounds. Sr. Mary joined the Kinsale community in 1957. . Having completed her teacher training at Carysfort College, Dublin, she taught in St.Joseph's primary school for thirty-six years, for twenty-three of which she was principal. She retired amid great pomp and circumstance in July 2000. It was clear from the celebrations that she was a much-loved teacher and principal. The talented and gentle Sr.DeLourdes Hegarty is the only Sister now in the school teaching the infants. The first lay principal is Mrs. Susan O'Hanrahan.

Sr. Mary loves the Convent Chapel, she has memories of her family coming for her Final Profession which was held in the chapel. She remembers many happy Community and family gatherings and of course the retreats which were held in the Chapel. Fr Redmond, a young Jesuit who led the community retreat when she was a young nun, had a profound effect on her. *"I remember some of his sayings and quotations, especially -"I am the Way the Truth and the Life" – I often come back to it in my prayer. It is a great source of comfort when I kneel and pray in the chapel."*

With her usual sense of humour she remembers another retreat priest who in order to make or emphasise a point would leap over the altar rails and pace up and down the chapel!

She remembers funeral celebrations, sad and joyous occasions celebrating the long lives of so many of the Sisters who are buried here in the convent cemetery and of course who will be left behind when the Community moves to its new home in Winter's Hill.

The whole community taken in 1976, celebrating Sr. Agnes Beary's Silver Jubilee

The old cemetery

The new cemetery

Niamh McEvoy, a twelve-year-old sixth class student at St. Joseph's Primary School penned this tribute to her school.

"I have many happy memories of my years in St.Joseph's, a few of which I will share with you.

I moved to Kinsale from Co.Clare at the very end of Senior Infants and was made to feel at home by Sr.De Lourdes and everybody from the start.

I remember being in a play called "The Sad Clown" at the school concert when I was seven and I really enjoyed it. It was my first time on stage and I still remember it vividly.

A few years later, a poet came to my school and shared with us lots of his poems. These poems really inspired me.

Sr.De Lourdes taught me both about music and about God when I was very young. A lot of her words have stuck with me for years. She and Sr.Mary McAuliffe taught me about kindness to the people less fortunate than we were and encouraged me to give to the missions. I also learned meditation with Sr.Mary.

Here is a list of services provided for the students:

Speech and drama, swimming, ballet, line dancing, Irish dancing, football, camogie, piano, tin whistle and Religious Education.

Not only did I learn about Maths and English, my school has allowed me to grow inside too, to follow God and respect other people."

The Pope visited Ireland in 1979. This was a wonderful occasion, a dream come true for so many of the Sisters. They went to the Phoenix Park, Galway, Knock and Limerick to see the Holy Father.

Huge changes were afoot within the Mercy Order. Meetings were being attended, discussions taking place and facilitators helping chart the way forward as all the Mercy Convents of the Cork and Ross Diocese prepared for their amalgamation.

Sister Immaculata Murphy was elected the first Mother General. There was a wonderful liturgical celebration at the South Parish Church in Cork, followed by a feast at the Convent of Mercy, St.Maries of the Isle. Four Sisters, to be known as "The Council", were elected to help Sr.Immaculata with her duties and with the smooth running of the congregation. They were Sister Clare McCarthy, Kinsale, Sister M.Mercy, (Imelda) St.Maries of the Isle, Sister M.Dolores, (Shiela) Bantry and Sister M.de Pazzi, St.Maries of the Isle.

All other offices ceased with these elections. Only the Sister Superior and the Bursars were to remain in place until the necessary changes could be made. In the spring of 1985 the new

Officers were appointed. This marked the movement from convent to convent, an entrance of new Sisters to Kinsale and the exit of many so well known and loved by the locals. It has worked well, as the Sisters who came in 1985 are no longer "new" and have won the hearts of the natives.

Sister de Lourdes Hegarty came from Passage West as superior of the Kinsale Community and Sister Colette from St.Maries of the Isle came as Bursar.

Sister Carmel Meaney went to be in charge of the convent at Ballindeasig.

Sister Carmel preceded Sister Mary McAuliffe as Principal of the Primary School, and is remembered by many former pupils who took part competitively and with great success in Irish Plays. Her work with the senior citizens, a ministry she took on after her retirement from school, is still carried on in the town.

Sister Mary O'Donoghue (Berchmans) headed for the city as Superior of St.Maries of the Isle.

Sister Joseph Keohane went to take charge of the Industrial School in Passage West.

Sister Gabriel Sweeney went west as Principal of the Primary School in Clonakilty and subsequently became Principal of Schull Primary School. She still lives and teaches in Schull. She recalls happy times in Kinsale.

"My first experience of Kinsale in Autumn 1956 was that of a shy, bewildered 13 year old going so far away from home for the first time, but I soon found care, kindness and friendship among both the Sisters and my classmates. Indeed my five boarding school years were happy years and when it came to autumn 1961, after quite some thought, talk and reflection, I decided to enter the Novitiate on "The Ramparts".

Even though Convent life had a very definite regime and rules were quite strict at that time, yet we, novices, had a lot of fun and with my novice companion at the piano, I'm sure there were evenings when our music, song and dance floated on the air towards Hogan's Row. On Summer afternoons at 1pm we – armed with a small yellow and white portable radio, crafts, reading material and sometimes a tin of dessert – betook ourselves around the hill to whichever one of our fields had the best view of Kinsale Harbour, and there we chatted, listened to "Dear Frankie" , knit, sewed, embroidered, etc. until 4pm.

A line from Grey's Elegy:

"The lowing herd winds slowly o'er the lea" comes to mind when I recall that at 4 PM we all retraced our steps to the Convent for afternoon tea followed by Vespers. Right now the word that encapsulates the above for me is "Carefree".

1965-1971 were study- plus -teaching years. This was hard work but very rewarding. In 1971 with study days behind me, my apostolate was now that of teaching for my remaining years in Kinsale, until 1985 when Diocesan Amalgamation was "new" and I was asked if I would take on Principalship of the Convent of Mercy Primary School in Clonakility.

Reflecting briefly on my years in Kinsale I know that they were enriching and that I was given every possible chance - so it is with gratitude and appreciation that I reflect; and I also know that although it is now nearly sixteen years since I left Kinsale, I still can walk in the Convent door any day or any night and experience a really homely welcome. That will never die."

Sister Clare McCarthy went as Principal to Mount Mercy Secondary School in Cork and made her home in Bishopstown. Sister Mary O'Donovan came from Skibbereen to replace her as Principal of Our Lady of the Rosary School.

Staff and children loved Sr.Clare, for her shrewd evaluation of situations and for her sense of fair play. Being a very creative person herself the arts thrived during her time as Principal. Here she reminisces on her early experience in Kinsale.

Kinsale 1959-1985

"September 1959: My first memory is of arriving with my family in Market Street, Kinsale and gazing up at the then impressive building overlooking the town, but being unable to navigate our way to it. Father O'Riordan, who happened to be passing by, gave us directions.

Inside, we were greeted in the front parlour, -the original site where Mercy began in Kinsale in 1844, and the room where it all began for me,- by Mother Imelda and Sr.Agatha.

Kinsale Convent would be my dwelling place –as a boarder until 1962 and as a Sister until 1985.

Novitiate days began on September 24th 1962. These were days of preparation for a life "set apart from the world,"prior to the influence of Vatican 2. My morning duty was to dust and polish the community room with Sr.Raphael, then a senior Sister. Here I met a nun, who had preserved her natural touch. "When you enter the convent, darling" she kindly advised me, "cultivate a duck's back." She certainly had done that. When she sprightly entered the community room on a Saturday morning in her high-heeled suede shoes and a glow of rouge on her cheeks I knew that she was off for a few hours "skite". Meticulously I would dust every crevice of woodwork, both high and low, and wax the large wooden floor with home-made wax and a leaden brush. Then with the electric polisher, I would bring the floor to a sparkling shine. Sisters were not allowed to run in those days, so no danger of one slipping on the polished floor! No wonder then, that the community room is still one of the best preserved rooms in the Convent!! Beneath that beautiful carpet lies a wooden floor that has been very well preserved.

There were nine of us in the novitiate, where the message of life was "Be ye perfect, as your Heavenly Father is perfect." This was guaranteed if "we did the ordinary things extraordinarily well." One thing we developed was a great camaraderie and we had lots of fun within the simple life-style. A favourite night, i.e. between eight and nine o'clock, was the night when Mother Oliver, our novice mistress, had an early rest, and Sister Regina took to the piano in the novitiate and we would dance to our hearts' content for an hour. Sr.Regina had entered in her forties and so brought a special something to the group. "Cheer up" she would say, "we'll soon be dead". She missed her cigarette and her car in her new chosen way of life, and perhaps she was consoling herself that her "reward" would be in heaven.

Back from College in 1968 and a "fully fledged" nun after my final profession on that same year, my years were now spent in Our Lady of the Rosary Secondary School. In those early days Primary and Secondary school pupils filled the rooms in the building to the right of the chapel. Here youth with their lively fresh spirit emanated a joy and exuberance which were palpable. Just opposite the main door was "Marymount", the staff room which often brimmed with fun and laughter at the eleven o'clock break, where Sr.Angela's brown bread was truly appreciated. Back in the classroom teachers and pupils plied with the books. However, the spirit and liveliness of the students was best captivated on the tennis courts, volleyball and soccer pitches, school operettas, gym displays, school debates, public speaking, charity walks, school tours –particularly to the Ring of Kerry or the Dingle Peninsula; and most of all at the school disco where we, teachers, kept guard and served burcos of water to the sound of music. Yes, to retreat to the convent and chat and share with community friends in the refectory or to spend quiet time in the chapel – a hallowed space- was balm to my spirit.

Life in that large building was enriching and fulfilling. Its walls and ramparts hold so many memories for me. Outside were the glorious and breathtaking views of Kinsale Harbour. The school day over, my favourite pastime was to take a walk around Compass Hill or over the Lower Road, or down the World's End and over the bridge to the Dock. To do so as the darkening sky was inflamed in a myriad of hues to the fading rays of the sinking sun was truly re-creation of body, mind and spirit. The beauty of Kinsale captivated me "the town I loved so well";(and a real heartache to leave it in 1985 when we joined diocesan union and I made my way to Bishopstown,Cork.) Like an anchor in my memory, it is held in place by the many people who journeyed with me, and who touched my life, during those endearing years....I have so much to be grateful for. Kinsale had been home to me for twenty-six years – formative years, nourishing years, fulfilling years. Its beauty, its people, St.Joseph's Convent, all have etched a very special niche in the recesses of my mind.... The gift of memory.

With deep affection and appreciation I revisit those Kinsale times – "those were happy days, in so many ways" and I share them with you as a token of gratitude and wish all at St.Joseph's *many memorable days in their new home."*

Sister Gerard, who had spent many years in the Sacred Heart Hospital, Kinsale went to Skibbereen and Sister Martina came from Skibbereen to replace her.

Sister Patricia Quinlan came from Passage West to teach in the Secondary School, where no doubt she caused much hilarity in the staffroom. Sister is now retired from school and is doing sterling work keeping the archives up to date and making the work of research so much easier for those of us fortunate enough to gain access to the diligently kept archives.

Sister Patricia reflects on her new home

"I will never forget the warm welcome extended to me by every member of the Kinsale Community when I was transferred here after spending most of my religious life in Passage West.

It made the transition so much easier and even the people of the town often stopped me and hoped I would be very happy in my new home

At that time I knew little of the story of Kinsale but I soon realised the rich history of the town and the contribution which the Sisters of Mercy had made in its development. The Sisters too were quick to acknowledge the debt they owed to the people of Kinsale for their support and help at all times.

Another thing that delighted me was the friendly relations that existed between the different religions in the town.

I can truly say the years I have spent here are among the happiest of my life."

In 1985 Sister Eileen McSweeney, a temporary professed Sister from St.Maries of the Isle, Cork came to teach Science in the Secondary School. Sr.Patricia and Sr.Eileen provided a meeting place for the young people of the town by initiating a "Discovery Group"every Monday night. Sister Eileen made her Final Profession in the Parish Church on August 11th 1987; the year Kinsale won the Tidy Towns' competition! In 1989 she went to work in Eldama Ravine, Kenya. She spent three and a half years ministering there before moving to Clonakilty, where she is a Science teacher and runs a private counselling practice. She is also a part-time lecturer at University College Cork.

About this time many of the Sisters reverted to their baptismal names, some from choice and others who as a result of amalgamation found themselves in Communities with Sisters of the same name.

Sister M.Regina, beloved of so many, died quite suddenly, causing great sadness. She is fondly remembered, by her Community and teaching colleagues as well as by the many children she taught.

In 1990 the Sisters were once again in conclave for the election of a new Mother General, Sister Immaculata having completed her term of office. This time the lot fell to Sr.Imelda O'Shaughness (Mercy) with Sister Mary O'Donoghue as First Councillor.

Sister Kevin O'Brien came from Bantry to replace Sister De Lourdes Hegarty as Superior. She had the good fortune of being Superior in the year the Convent celebrated its 150th anniversary in 1994. She has this to say:

"There is quite a lot of reference to "heritage" and going back to our roots, etc. Here in Kinsale we have a very rich heritage of Mercy. John O'Donoghue's quote comes to mind "Tá Tír na n-Óg ar chúl an tighe."

I came to Kinsale in 1991 with some apprehension. Leaving Bantry for me was a big "letting go," having "let go" of Clonakilty five years previously. My fears were soon forgotten with the warm Mercy welcome I received in Kinsale, and acceptance, which is very important to someone coming in as an outsider.

I had the privilege of being involved in the preparation for the 150th anniversary of the coming of the Sisters to Kinsale, which was celebrated in April 1994. During the preparations and going through the Annals I was deeply impressed and inspired by the vision and generosity of the Sisters at that time in sending labourers into the vineyard to so many different parts of the world – a true missionary spirit.

Hurrah for the Sisters of Mercy, Kinsale.

I quote in full Sister Patricia Quinlan's account of the Celebrations of the 150th anniversary.

"A paean of praise and thanksgiving to God rose to my lips as I looked out of my window on a morning of glorious sunshine on April 16th, when 150 years of dedicated service to the people of Kinsale and district by the Sisters was to be publicly honoured by a day of celebration. After a week of incessant rain and drizzle was it any wonder I felt like singing: "O, what a beautiful Morning, O, what a beautiful day"? !

Celebrations began at 2.30pm when 25 priests concelebrated Mass in the Parish Church of St.John the Baptist. The main celebrants were Most Rev.Dr. Buckley, Bishop of Cork and Ross, Fr.Jeremiah Hyde, P.P. and Very Rev. Dr. Carthach McCarthy, Chaplain to the Convent. Fr Ted Hallihane proved an excellent M.C. and his many days of tireless preparation ensured that everything went without a hitch.

The homily was given by Diocesan Historian, Sr.Angela Bolster, and the round of applause at the end showed how much the people appreciated it. Many of them were stunned by the amount of work accomplished by the Sisters over the years.

The choir of Our Lady of The Rosary School conducted by Miss Mary Lordan, their music teacher, was a credit to her expertise, and the soloists, Yvonne O'Sullivan, Sister Mary

O'Donoghue and Donal McDonnell, Vice-Principal of the school, won universal praise.

All aspects of the Convent including its schools, hospital and support groups were presented in the Offertory Procession to the accompaniment of Kevin Goggin on the violin.

At the end Sr.Kevin O'Brien thanked all who had contributed in any way to make the Sacred Liturgy so meaningful and invited everyone to refreshments in the Convent. Many fond memories were recalled as Past Pupils met after many years, some as far back as the 1940's. Among the guests was Walter Bridgeman, a direct descendant of Mother Mary Francis Bridgeman.

Huge crowds walked through the Convent, some to admire the newly decorated Church or enjoy the sun in the garden, to congratulate the Centenarians or to gaze in admiration and browse over the wonderful display of the convent History, truly a work of art, produced by Sr.M.de Lourdes Hegarty.

I met an old man of 92 years and his wife at the very top of the house and he said he had yearned to see what was up there from the time he was an altar boy in the Convent!

The visitors enjoyed a Recital by the band of the Southern Command under Colonel Tom Murphy, who hails from Kinsale. This took place on the green of Acton's Hotel, and while listening to the beautiful strains of the Marina Waltz, etc. the people could view the beauty of the harbour, thanks to the efficient traffic control carried out by the Gardai.

Pupils from the Primary and Secondary Schools provided a Guard of Honour for the unveiling of the monument to the Sisters on the pier.

The Rector of Kinsale, Rev.David Williams, read a sea-faring prayer and Bishop Buckley blessed and unveiled the monument which bore the inscription: "Erected by the pupils, past and present, staff and friends to commemorate 150 years of dedicated service by the Sisters of Mercy 1884 – 1994. For me to live is Christ – St.Paul."

This is a beautiful stone and timber monument with an engraving of the Convent building, which will also serve as a waterfront seat for the public on a site donated by Kinsale Harbour Commissioners.

Sr.Kevin O'Brien thanked the P.P.U. and organising committee and said the generosity shown was an indication of the close links between Sisters and pupils, past and present. She concluded with very appropriate lines from her favourite poet, Patrick Kavanagh:

"O commemorate me where there is water.
Commemorate me beautifully with a seat for the passer-by".

All then adjourned to Actons Hotel for a meal and many special presentations were made to Sr.Kevin on behalf of the Sisters. These included a magnificent framed pen and watercolour drawing of Kinsale Convent by Patricia Lordan, a past pupil, and a certificate of appreciation and coat of arms presented by Dermot Collins, Chairperson of Kinsale U.D.C. Donal McDonnell presented Sr.Kevin with Kinsale Crystal on behalf of the staff, while Bob Quinn, manager of A.I.B. Bank Kinsale, presented a framed new £5 featuring Mother McAuley. There was also a framed message of congratulations from President Mary Robinson and a congratulatory message from the English Ambassador to Ireland whose Sisters of Mercy, from Derby were present. Many more tributes and presentations were received, all of which Sr.M.Kevin graciously received, and she smilingly thanked the donors in her own calm, inimitable way.

A former orphan at the Convent brought a tear to the eye of everyone in Actons Hotel with a few simple sentences. She told of the happy childhood she and her five sisters had at the convent; the Sisters gave her a home, they gave her love when she had no one else. She got a standing ovation from the huge crowd present. Another orphan, now a Sister in England wrote: "The Kinsale Sisters gave us what money could not buy; love and a good start in life. What always stands out in my mind is that we were always praised for our slightest achievement and made to feel special. I cannot recall one unkind word or even gesture in the fourteen and a half years with them."

It certainly was a day to remember, and I feel we have much to learn from those dedicated Sisters who went before us. May God reward them for their devoted service to Him."

The late Frank Hurley, who was the first male teacher to join the staff at Our Lady of the Rosary School, and whose commitment and loyalty to the Sisters over the years is legendary, produced a book to mark this happy occasion. It is a wonderful book

Celebrating 150 years of Mercy in Kinsale. It is simply called – "St. Joseph's Convent of Mercy, Kinsale" and contains wonderful photographs of fellow pupils, Sisters and friends whom we recognise, as well as accounts of the Industrial school, lace making, and the Sisters in the Crimea plus many more interesting and informative articles. It was launched on the day of the celebrations and is still available from bookshops in the town.

Sr Elma Coakley presenting a copy of Frank's book to President Mary McAleese

Now more changes are afoot. A Chapter was held in 1995 to decide whether the Cork and Ross Sisters were ready or willing to join "Mercy Ireland". With decreasing numbers this seemed a practical idea. Each Province would have its own Leadership team, which would be answerable to a Central team in Dublin. Mercy convents had always been autonomous. This was the wish of Catherine McAuley – A local Convent serving a local community – and of course over the years wonderful links were forged between the convents and the local community. Even with dwindling numbers this was a mega change and needed much prayer, deliberation and an ever-increasing attendance at meetings. This must have thrown many of the ageing Sisters into confusion.

However Mercy Ireland came to pass and with it further restructuring. Two major changes within such a short time demanded amazing resilience.

1995 and it was again time for what is now being called a Provincial Chapter. Sister Colette was elected Provincial at this Chapter with Sr.Ena O'Donovan, Sr.Mary O'Donoghue, Sr. Maria McGuinness, Sr.Coirle McCarthy and Sr.Miriam Kirrisk as her Councillors.

Around this time a decision was made by the Council which was to cause pain and distress to many of the Senior, and not so Senior, Sisters at Kinsale. That was the decision to close St.Josephs and build a new Convent, further around Winters Hill. This began a bitter process for the Sisters as they tried to come to terms with the closing of the Convent founded by Mother Mary Ann Burke in 1844. To this Convent on the hill so many Sisters had come over the years; also many had left to found new Convents and begin a new life in their chosen mission, many of them never saw Kinsale again. Then there were those of us who left to return to lay life and make our way in the world which had changed so much in the years we had been in Kinsale. For many of us who left Kinsale Convent has always been a haven to which we could return and be given a warm welcome.

Sister Eleanor made the following contribution, which reflects the feelings of many of the Sisters.

"Will it be 2000 or 2001? This question is often heard in my home nowadays. For some, mostly those for whom St.Josephs has been their home from their late teens or early twenties, it is asked with apprehension. For others, mostly those who did not join the Mercy Order in Kinsale, a sense of anticipation pervades. The "it" of course, refers to the movement from our home on the Ramparts to our new one on Winters Hill. Let us hope that the name was not derived from the season!

A distinct honour for me is that I am, the last inhabitant who both came to the building as a postulant and will leave it for our new home, having spent almost a quarter of the life of the building in it. That quarter consists of a past, a present and hopes for the future.

The past involved a Novitiate full of activities some of which I loved; singing, piano and elocution (Irish and English), crotchet, spiritual reading, meditation, doing honours maths. Latin and maths-physics for the leaving certificate and going to U.C.C. and some of which I hated; dusting, polishing, cleaning and sewing.

It was a rich time behaviourally, emotionally, socially and spiritually. This richness was in no small way provided by the twelve others who were there when I joined up. Our friendship helped us explore real issues. I can remember discussions on which vow was the hardest! This of course changed considerably over time. As with all groups, there were the shadow sides – the jealousies and rivalries which for the most part remained covert.

The present is both rich and sad. As a full time professor in U.C.C., I embrace a surprising number of tasks, lecturing, research, training and supervising counsellors, being a member of the Governing body and Academic Council. Taking up my position at the University emerged into my life when some staff of the Department at the time approached me on three occasions to apply. At this time the nicest Superior of my life thus far, Sr.Immaculata Murphy, said "If God wishes you to be there, you will get it, if not, you will not." Such Faith filled orientation convinced me completely. In 1981 I became a fulltime member of staff."

The new building will not hold the precious memories and the volume of history. Neither will it contain the beautiful features of the existing building – The Chapel Ceiling, The elegant Community Room, spacious gardens and gently winding staircase. "If only the walls could

speak" – the present Convent has seen so much joy and so much sorrow as the Community strove to meet the ever changing needs of generations of families of Kinsale. It has been the one 'constant' in the changing fortunes of so many families, giving that sense of continuity and forging strong links with families in the town.

Having celebrated with the Sisters we must also grieve with them. It is now known that moving house is one of the most traumatic experiences of our life. Think what it must be like for these ladies who are leaving behind 157 years' history in what has always been a flagship of the Mercy Congregation. The Sisters, like their role model the humble Carpenter who had no place on which to lay His head, will make the transition to their new home, with our love, prayers and support, and they will continue "to bloom where they are planted."

Fr Myles McSweeney, Kinsale's youngest and newest curate has penned this beautiful poem, to celebrate this "closure" in the lives of the Sisters.

Moving On

Memories flow like a flood on the floor
As she opens the chapel door.
How often has she come in here?
Through years of toil and fear.

Now her work is done.
Heaven waiting to be won,
As she opens her office
Remembering the days she was a novice.

Sixty years in the same stall,
Ever faithful to her call.
Many have come and gone,
But still she prays on.

Going back over years of faces

Who are now in so many places.

Sr. Pauline, Sr. Michael, Sr. James

As she holds her beads like reins.

Now it's time to move on

The past is gone.

The future is unfolded,

In a new house being moulded.

Hail Mary, full of grace,

How will I leave this place?

O Mother, for you I will

For I trust your mercy still.

Vatican Council Two 1963 – 1965

Perfectae Caritatis: Decree on the appropriate renewal of Religious life.

Religious women and men were asked "to reflect seriously and actively so as to discover how their institute could and should be adapted ever more perfectly to the continuously changing circumstances of their times."

There were two fundamental norms highlighted as to the direction which change and reformation should take:

1.The following of Christ as set down in the Gospels and

2.That each order would reflect the individual spirit of the founder.

We know that without change there can be no growth, we will die and we also know that change is painful.

The founders were very much people of their time. We know how Catherine McAuley met the needs of the poor and the sick of nineteenth century Dublin. The question for the Mercy Congregation now is "where would we find her today, to whom would she commit all her energy and her considerable wealth?"

According to the decree for Religious, keeping the rules is less important than living the spirit of the rules. "The Sabbath was made for man, not man for the Sabbath."

We live in astonishing times, so much has changed in the forty years since the Vatican Council. Meeting contemporary needs in the light of the Gospel is a huge challenge.

Change of course needs to come from the inside out, the renewal of spirit giving life to the external changes.

A life consecrated by the profession of the evangelical counsels – the vows of poverty, chastity and obedience – is of surpassing value and has a very necessary role to play in the circumstances of the present age. Communities, according to Vatican Council Two should retain their own special character and purpose.

Combining the zeal of an apostle with wise judgements made in the light of faith concerning the circumstances of the modern world, they will be able to come to the aid of people more effectively (Vat.2.)

Contemplation combined with apostolic love is, I think the key. Bringing the feminine qualities of intuition and nurturing will help Religious to act with compassion and in a non-judgemental way.

Chapter 6
Personal Recollections

St.Joseph's Convent of Mercy holds precious memories for a wide variety of people - Sisters, teachers, students, parents and townspeople. This chapter is devoted to the reflections, anecdotes, memories and humour of such people

Eugene Gillan, a man generous with his time and talents was a lighthouse keeper for many years around the Irish coast. He has a long association with the Sisters, first as a parent - his children Sally, Mandy, Cearma, Igan and Gerard attended the Primary and Secondary Schools - and as an artist as we read in the following:

The House with the Golden Windows.

As I recall my association with the Convent of Mercy, my memories go back to the days when I travelled to the town from the Old Head of Kinsale. I would meet the girls from the Convent walking in groups on the World's End road. They would have nuns walking with them. They gave me the impression that they were happy young people.

As the years went by, I came back to Kinsale to make my own home with children of my own. They became pupils at the Convent. At that time I was working in Northern Ireland and had to stay for a month at work followed by a month's holiday in Kinsale. I used to dabble at painting in these remote but beautiful places on the coasts of Donegal, Derry and Antrim. During one of my holiday periods my daughter Sally asked if I would help paint the scenery for the musical being staged at the Convent school.

I was introduced to Sister Francis who explained what was required. Frank Buckley was producer of the operetta. My first task was to locate the canvasses under the stage. They were in poor condition and had to be cleaned and repaired. The Sisters and pupils worked hard to have them ready. While I was painting, Frank was rehearsing and the pupils had to walk around the painted canvasses which were on the floor of the hall. On a number of occasions they would walk on the canvas sometimes by accident, sometimes a prank. Frank's blood pressure would, I imagine go very high. The boys and girls enjoyed the last minute panic. On that occasion we just managed to have the back drops in place for the opening night but some of the paint was still wet. All of the girls and boys on stage had quite a bit of paint on their costumes, not to mention Frank himself and Sr. Francis. Needless to say tempers were frayed.

I was glad to be off to peaceful Donegal but everyone enjoyed the production.

Next year came along. Sr. Francis with Frank approached me again. We had a council to see what we would do. I explained to Frank that I would need new material to hang and that I would need plenty of time. Sr. Francis and myself made a number of trips to Cork to purchase new canvas, paint and brushes. The boys and girls made humourous remarks about these trips. I had hoped to paint the scenes on the stage but that was not possible, so back to the hall floor again, with the usual results -little footprints and handprints, all adding to the spirit of preparation.

During one of the productions the B.B.C. were filming in the Kinsale area. The film crew was based in the town. I had met with them on a previous occasion while in Northern Ireland. On the evening of the final rehearsals they called up to the convent for a chat about next day's filming. Here last minute preparations were in full swing. They came to the musical that night and enjoyed it. I thought, perhaps that they were just polite. Almost 30 years later, while in Cork, by chance I met the head of the production team who was very much involved in musical productions in the B.B.C. In the course of our conversation he mentioned the musical in Kinsale Convent. One of his fondest memories of Ireland was of that musical and the standard of music rendered by the pupils.

As the troubles in the North became worse, I had to spend more time away from Kinsale and my association with the Convent, the nuns, and the pupils became less and less. Unfortunately all that has passed and the hall is now silent. In the evening time as I look towards the Convent, the windows are gleaming in the setting sun. It reminds me of a story of long ago about "the house with the golden windows" The past pupils, I'm sure, must have golden memories, along with all the ups and downs of life in school. As the poet mentioned "he marveled at the sweetness in the sad and sadness in the sweet"

Our Lady of the Rosary School had been providing second level education in Kinsale since 1932 when it was established as a Secondary top. It became a Secondary School proper in 1952. Sister Baptist Molloy was the First Principal, and it was significant that while Sr.Baptist's funeral Mass was being said at the Convent Chapel, the final Mass for the students of Our Lady of the Rosary was being said at the Parish Church. The students returned to the Convent to form a Guard of Honour for the former Principal as her coffin was carried to the little cemetery in the Convent garden. The following principals succeeded Sr.Baptist: Sr.Augustine Treacy, Sr.Regina Sheehan, Sr.Clare McCarthy (Francis) and Sr.Mary O'Donovan.

The school opened its doors to boys in 1968, one of the first convent schools to do so. This was due to the vision of the then Principal Sr.Augustine Treacy.

Donal McDonell retired as Vice Principal of the School in July 2001. A post he held with pride and competence for 24 years, supporting each Principal with his hard work and sound advice. He brought his own brand of humour and wisdom to the school and all who worked and studied therein for over thirty years.

"I started work in Holy Rosary School in September 1968 under Sr.Augustine Treacy the then Principal. Her vision and foresight always impressed me. She had built the hall - which incorporated a fully equipped gymnasium - a new science laboratory and additional classrooms. The school had just become co-educational.

Sr.Francis (Clare) McCarthy was a young and dynamic Principal. During her time the subject ranges were increased, and to accommodate the increase in pupil numbers the old primary school rooms were taken over. A Career Guidance teacher was introduced into the educational system during that time.

The Annual operetta was one of the many highlights of the school year and was always a professional performance on the night.

The annual school sports were always keenly contested and very enjoyable, with students and teachers participating and parents involved as well.

The Debs/Grads Ball was introduced during this time and has continued successfully to date.

Working out the school timetable was a one to two week headache - with so many permutations and combinations before the final product was ready - all without the aid of computers in the early days.

Games, outdoor pursuits, school tours, etc. always enjoyed by students and staff. Great stories still abound about these events.

Final examination results always greeted with laughter, tears and screams - a time of great excitement.

The school discos enjoyed immensely by the students but - dare I say it - a nightmare for the teachers who had to supervise them!

Sr.Mary O'Donovan followed Sr.Francis McCarthy as School Principal and continued the good work. Sr.Mary was faced with the enormous task of promoting and supervising the building of the new Community School. This challenge she undertook with enthusiasm and diligence, and as a result of her "friendly persuasion" of the Department of Education, we now have the Kinsale Community School.

During my time in Kinsale I always enjoyed meeting the parents at the Parent-Teacher meetings and had many long chats about past pupils.

My friend and colleague Frank Hurley's untimely death sent shock waves through the school - a wonderful person in every way - to this day his name is frequently mentioned within the staff-room."

Donal McDonnell presenting a crystal vase on behalf of the staff to Sr.Kevin O'Brien on the 150th anniversary of the Convent.

Vera O'Herlihy, a true Kinsale girl belonging to a large and well known family in the town, attended St.Joseph's Infant and Primary School as well as the Holy Rosary Secondary School to which she returned to teach P.E. in the nineteen sixties. One could say she was there from the age of four until her retirement! She was the first Physical Education teacher in the secondary school and is a hard act to follow. Many a past pupil will no doubt appreciate her commitment, creativity and the joy and enthusiasm she brought to her subject.

"The convent for me always had an air of mystery, a secret stillness, a place of peace, yet full of fun with all its nooks and crannies.

I started my education there at the age of four, continued through secondary school and returned there as physical education teacher in 1968. I have very happy memories of the many years spent at the Convent School and also some sad ones. Our staffroom was always full of laughter and good humour. Our late great colleague and friend, Frank Hurley, always had some new venture or story to brighten even the darkest days of winter. Colleagues were always ready to listen, lend a hand, give advice and there was a great feeling of working together. Subjects were creatively linked and dance, music, religion, art French, history etc. all intertwined with great involvement in local events. One of these events which comes to mind was the dance drama portraying the flight of the Wild Geese. Sister Gertrude and myself spent many happy warm sunny days working with a great team of students on the pontoon at the Trident. Fr.Brian

Kelly taped the haunting Irish airs and gave the narration, and the performance was done at night with lighted torches, the Wild Geese departing the pontoon, leaving behind a broken hearted Mise Eire portrayed beautifully by Alex Fitzgerald (Archer).

The school was always full of music. The dedication and interest of Sister Kieran in her subject echoed through the Convent, as child after child softly played their piece on the piano. The operas produced by Frank Buckley were of outstanding quality as was the forty strong orchestra.

With the drive and far sightedness of Sr.Augustine and the support of Mother Baptist we succeeded in getting a fully equipped gym for the school when few schools had one. Displays were performed both indoors and outdoors, and a group of very talented students performed at the Mansion House in Dublin.

Another great venture was the purchasing of a boat for the school. It was always my dream that the students would have the opportunity of experiencing life on the water. Thanks to the great support of Sr.Francis (Clare McCarthy) this dream became a reality, and for many years children who had never put foot in a boat experienced the thrill of rowing or motoring out the harbour.

Sr Columba R.I.P.

The summer term brought with it its own magic - the colourful splash of flowers in the Convent garden; the Quarant Ore procession with the lovely hymns wafting softly on the air. Donal McDonell's rendering of Panis Angelicus; Sr.Columba and Rossie, her faithful sheepdog, wending their way past the orchard to the farm; the awe of the town students as a cow gave birth to a calf below the tennis courts; kids racing each other to get to the tennis courts for the school tournaments and the excitement of visiting teams; and the older nuns sitting quietly meditating on the veranda. These for me, are wonderful memories of warm sunny days full of learning and happiness.

However, change is inevitable and when the school was condemned Sr.Mary succeeded in procuring the beautifully situated Community School high above the Marsh. The Secondary School closed its doors. The patter of footsteps on the flag passage was no longer heard. Song sinks into silence, all is quiet.

"As up the Convent Walls in golden streaks

The ascending sunbeams mark the days decrease;

And as he asks what there the stranger seeks

Thy voice along the cloisters whispers "Peace"

(Longfellow)

Alexandra Archer (nee Fitzgerald) mentioned by Vera in the previous passage was an excellent dancer and gymnast. The ease with which she moved was a joy to behold. In the following "piece" she recalls her own memories of happy days spent in both schools.

Memories of the Convent.

"My earliest memories of the old convent centre around the babies classroom and my first teacher, Sr.Mary Rose. I can still hear her musical voice and the sound of the piano in the corner and recall the small inkwelled desks where we sat listening and watching her arms moving amid the voluminous folds of her habit.

Later in fifth and sixth class it was the neat figure of Sr.Mary Patrick who held sway over the classroom. She was the chief inspiration behind the operettas that were produced each year in the school hall. To this day those lovely melodies evoke the magic and excitement of these shows. Little did I know when I sang and swept in "Thumbelina" that I would be back on that same stage a generation later singing with Kinsale Opera and choreographing the Secondary School's production of "The Boyfriend."

The Convent was above all, a place of reverence and prayer and I have treasured memories of times spent in the beautiful chapel and in the quiet stillness of that place marvelling at the transformation of the light as it passed through the stained glass windows and was reflected off the painted and polished surfaces. I remember too the peacefulness of the gardens during outdoor prayers where the only sound among so many children, was that of the breeze rustling through the rosebeds.

In my garden there is a rosebush given to me by Sr.M.Rose. It blooms every year and its blossoms are red. I do not know its name, nor why she gave it to me. All I know is that it is a beautiful inheritance. In ways like this and so many others the old Convent will live in the hearts of all of us who remember it so fondly."

Rosie Cargin, not to be outdone by her younger sister Alex! has volunteered her own memories of her integration into life at the Convent as a Leaving Cert. Student. Clearly she brought her own unique gift of friendship to the students she joined.

"When I was fifteen my parents returned to Ireland after many years away and decided to settle in Kinsale. I was sent back to the English school to finish O'Levels and then went to the Convent of Mercy for the Leaving Certificate year.

The Convent building looked austere to me but it was a short and pleasant walk from our house on Compass Hill. I set off that soft early September morning passed Mr.O'Dell and his dog at the top to St.John's Hill and waved to Mrs.James in her garden at Rampart House. I was feeling somewhat doubtful about the prospect of joining a class whose members had probably known one another since infancy, but I had a survival plan: if I didn't like it I wouldn't go back after the lunch break!

The ascetic appearance of the outer fabric belied the warm welcoming atmosphere and the colourful mixture of personalities that I encountered within. The sixth year classroom was sunny, with well-worn wooden desks and chairs. I found a seat beside Teresa Murphy and nearby sat Donal Goggin, Mary Assumpta Kelleher and Collette Jelley.

I liked my classmates and they put me at ease from the start. The nearest I came to feeling the "blow-in" that I was came when someone asked me if I thought I would "ever lose that English accent"! Likewise I found the cadences of Cork an intriguing novelty!

Naturally the nuns were figures of authority to us at that time and they certainly made us work. Every so often Sister Augustine would appear on the threshold of the classroom door when noise levels had surpassed the reasonable. Mother Albert's lessons made a vivid and lasting impression on me, particularly her exhortation to us to have "backbone" when travelling in taxis after parties with boys!

Humour was always part of school life. Most of the Sisters had been given nicknames by the pupils, but I had better not elaborate on that! Not withstanding such juvenile banter, there was always and atmosphere of respect, order and an unspoken acceptance of each person. It was not a rigid school. I remember sitting in the library and listening to the cleaner singing as she swept and polished the floors along those long corridors. The profound Christian Values that lay at the heart of the Convent and were expressed by the gentleness, dedication and kindness of the nuns underpinned everything that was done.

I did of course return after lunch that first day and have revisited the Convent several times since with my own children."

Mary Cooper (Murray) from Toames, Kilmichael, was a pupil of Holy Rosary School from 1966 - 1971 She is a G.P. in Pembrokeshire where she lives with her husband Peter and their three beautiful and talented daughters.

"I have very happy memories of my time in Kinsale. One of my earliest memories is of our class being asked to draw a flower. On the basis of our works of art, it was decided whether we would study Art or Latin. I was told firmly that I should do Latin - advice, with which I must say I totally agree! Art was never my strong point.

The emphasis was on producing well-rounded individuals rather than on the purely academic, Rules existed but were enforced in a humane way. Common sense often meant that a blind eye was turned on less serious misdemeanours.

During our last year in school, Kathleen Daly and I went down town every afternoon after school. It was our way of unwinding during our break time, and we came back for study relaxed and refreshed.

Kathleen and I had a very satisfactory (to us!) arrangement about homework. We both studied Latin (which I hated and she loved) and music (which she hated and I loved) for Intermediate Certificate. She did my Latin and I did her music, so we were both happy - though I am not so sure about our teachers.

One of the most valuable lessons I learned in Kinsale was my appreciation of music, and for this I have to thank Sr.Kieran. She showed me, for the first time, that music is a form of expression rather than a mechanical exercise. Sr.Dominic (Gertie McGrath) who taught me music for Leaving Cert. further deepened this appreciation. This love of music has stayed with me and enriched my life, and I like to think I have been able to pass it on to my children. I am also deeply grateful that I was able to do Music for Leaving Cert. - I was the only student in the class. I cannot imagine that many schools would now be able to offer this facility to a class of one!

Other memories come to mind - how I always managed to arrange my piano lessons during P.E. Miss Herlihy used to complain - but I rather think she must have been secretly relieved, as I would surely have won a prize for the most clumsy, physically inept pupil in the school.

Sr. Francis (now Sr.Clare McCarthy) is surely the best maths teacher ever, and I still feel it is a great tragedy that she is lost to the classroom - though no doubt doing very valuable work elsewhere.

Up to thirty five years later, it is difficult to bring back memories of other experiences and people who have undoubtedly influenced and benefited me, but I hope that these words help to convey my gratitude to all those who helped to make my years in Kinsale so happy and fruitful."

The following are the impressions and memories of Pat Holohan who taught at Our Lady of the Rosary School for thirty years. He was a well-loved colleague and teacher with a wonderful sense of humour.

"When I joined the staff in 1970, Vatican 11 and educational reforms had already encouraged both convent and school well forward on the road of change. I write of convent and school in the same sentence, advisedly, because the one mingled with the other, physically and

otherwise. To get from, say the laboratory to the home economics department one walked through the convent part of the long main building which looked down to the harbour like the citadel of an Italian hill-top town; one walked by the chapel, through the hall with its rope dangling from the stairwell, by the parlours, by the kitchen and through the dark, holy picture- lined corridor. From the kitchen came Sister Angela's brown bread or hot apple tart for the teachers' elevenses, and it would be to the residential side of the house that an ailing pupil would be sent to be fussed over by Mother Albert. One of the classrooms still kept its former name and was called the Chapel of Mary. No Roman took greater interest in a Papal Enclave than the staff took in the election of a new Reverend Mother.

The Late Mother Albert Treacy

The school calendar reflected the needs of the liturgy and religious life. The start of the Christmas holidays was sometimes decided by the timing of the Sisters' retreat. The tradition of the forty hours was observed, the entire school being assembled in the garden for the Procession after which Sister Fachtna presided over lunch for the male teachers in the library. At Easter a few of us made a dash to Upton to buy tulips for the altar. Convent life, however, was in transition and we noted the gradual changes in dress and the increasingly active role already being assumed by our religious colleagues in the new subject associations founded in response to curricular developments.

Free education and the school buses had encouraged more and more students to stay longer in education. The school had already admitted boys who, in 1970, however numbered only two in Leaving Cert. Gradually numbers of boys and girls increased, allowing the boarding school to be closed. Extra rooms in the old building were taken over especially when St.Joseph's N.S. moved to a new school.

The staff room occupied its own detached house. If memory serves, there were six lay teachers (three men and three women) on the staff when I arrived and the same number of Sisters. The Principal was Sister Augustine who had been responsible for much of the development which the school had already undergone. The staffroom was somewhat of a refuge from the rigours of teaching and an atmosphere of camaraderie reigned within it.

Sister Regina used to entertain us with the story of her last cigarette at the Grotto in Belgooly - she was a late vocation- and with tales of the dance floors of West Cork and Skibbereen *where she had begun her teaching career. Frank Hurley, animateur of the staffroom and much else, kept us in touch with the happenings in the town, and the days were few indeed when he did not have an amusing yarn for us. He had inexhaustible energy for his innumerable activities and he was blessed with a resilience and sense of humour which overcame every setback. His talent for mimicry and his gift for comic timing found expression in the school operas and in the productions of the local dramatic society, particularly in the more racy pantomime roles.*

The Late Frank Hurley

Sr Joan with Breda Eaton

Solas na BhFlaitheas air agus orthu siúd a d'imigh romhainn

Sisters Brendan, the late Sr.Kevin Ryan, the late Sr.Angela and Mary Myles preparing Christmas fare.

Louise, youngest of the seven Tobin children to attend both Convent schools reminisces on her time spent at the Ramparts.

"January 2001 and I am back in the Convent for my first return visit in several years. The occasion is a quiet celebration to mark the re-election to the Governing Body of UCC of my colleague, Sr. Eleanor O'Leary, Professor of Applied Psychology. It is appropriate that our host for the evening is a psychologist, for the return to the Convent is marked by all sorts of responses of memory. I am seated in the back parlour - a room I had rarely set foot in during my schooldays - and studying those timeless pictures on the wall and the deeper images of memory which have come flooding back.

Predictably, all the spaces I pass through seem smaller now - as they always do when one returns to childhood haunts. Yet the sweep of the central staircase is as majestic as ever and the chestnut floor tiles in the hall have retained their high gloss. Some days later I realise that I had forgotten all about that bell -pull by the stairs, that ingeniously personalised "paging " system which notified the nuns of the arrival of their visitors. As children, we were intrigued by the subtleties of this system which guaranteed such dignified social proprieties. (It is indeed a wonder that the system wasn't patented by the Order!)

The reason that all my recollections are so bound up with the physicality of the surroundings is that, for the best part of 13 years of my life, the Convent of Mercy was central to my existence and that of so many others who passed through its corridors. Looking back on it all now, I find it curious that as pupils we managed to spend so much of our time in the Convent quarters, considering that they were technically "out of bounds." We were instructed that we should use what was rather inelegantly described as the "back passage" when travelling from the main school building to faraway regions such as the music room, the gym, the tennis courts etc. But the lure of the prohibited Convent route was too much of a temptation for most of us and we generally made it our business to dart furtively along the inside walkway, interrupting our run to genuflect quickly in front of the chapel door, swiftly passing by the parlour and main staircase, until we were home and dry on that last stretch of corridor that led to the music room.

That exploration of the physical landscape of the Convent was part and parcel of the way we lived. The external topography of the grounds was equally significant for us; we loved nature walks in third and fourth class which brought us through the Convent gardens and up around Compass Hill. A highlight of these walks was the occasional sighting of the nuns' laundry hanging out to dry on the clothesline (prompting wisecracks that "these were nature walks alright " from the more daring among us.) Quarant Ore is another event etched in the memory - Maytime mysticism, suffused in the scent of incense. Along by the glasshouses we schoolgirls watched in envy as our brothers from St. John's ceremoniously strewed petals along the pathway.

My relationship with the Convent of Mercy began in 1966 when Sr. Mary Rose greeted us in "Babies". I was the seventh member of my family to pass through her hands. Older brothers - all four of whom had spent babies and sevenses in the Convent before moving on to St.John's - had sounded dire warnings about the punishment for misdemeanours which might await us - enforced imprisonment in a small room which we might now describe as an annex to a classroom but which we then called the coalhouse. Plunged into the benign atmosphere of Sr.Mary Rose's classroom, I think I felt mildly cheated that the disciplinary procedures I had heard all about did not, after all, materialise.

A particular feature of the early years was our preoccupation with the distinction between white veils and black veils. The white veils will, for me, forever be bound up with the exoticism of young nuns just returned from Florida to teach us. The veils changed altogether some years later and my recollection of the Landing on the Moon in 1969 is fused with the nuns' changeover to wimpleless headgear that very week.

I often wish I could regain in adult life the academic and social pinnacle which I reached in third and fourth class, taught by Sr. Mary De Lourdes McAuliffe, Even though we tried her patience with our pranks (we were a self -styled "Famous Five" at that time) my four pals and I could not fail to learn from this gifted and surprising teacher whose love of words instilled in me and others a lifelong interest in reading.

The transition to secondary was seamless for townies such as myself even if I and my comrades from sixth class took some time to warm to the boarders and bus commuters from unknown territories such as Ballingeary and Ballinspittal. However, tribal divisions were soon broken down once we were catapulted into the exciting world of gymnastics and volleyball. I doubt if any other school in Ireland had such a well -equipped sports hall at the time.

The late 1970s were a time of transition for the Mercy Order and many of the nuns decided to leave the Convent at that stage. This change marked the beginning of the new secularisation of the school and as young adults we were well tuned in to the changes that were taking place in Irish society. Yet, even if some of the teaching nuns had moved on, many of the familiar faces from other parts of the Convent staff remained and to this day offer irreplaceable community service to the town of Kinsale. I suppose Sr. Catherine springs immediately to mind; her contribution to the town has been enormous and I know of many people whom she has helped along the way. I wish her and all her sisters in the community many long and happy years in their new surroundings.

The Convent dominates the town of Kinsale and has had a major influence on many lives. I can only hope that, in its new incarnation, the Convent will continue its mission of serving the people of Kinsale.

Sr.Elma Coakley came as Superior to the Convent in 1994. She enjoyed her time there and still retains a good relationship with the Community, returning on regular visits.

When I was asked to go to Kinsale as leader, I got quite a shock and was very apprehensive about going there. However all my fears were soon allayed by the warm welcome I got, in particular from the senior Sisters. Sr.Albert thanked me publicly at a Community meeting for coming to them. What impressed me about the Kinsale Community was first of all their hospitality; no matter who came or at what time, they were always made welcome and given a beautiful meal. It didn't matter how many arrived, they always seemed to have plenty food to go around. One morning we entertained a whole busload of American Sisters and treated them to freshly baked scones and tea. The Sisters always spent time with visitors.

Another trait was the atmosphere of prayer. The choir was hardly ever without somebody at prayer, or Sisters Anne or Fachtnan praying the Rosary in the refectory. The older Sisters had a very deep prayer life.

I found great flexibility there and a freedom to come and go without being watched or questioned. During my time there we had several jubilees and celebrations, the most memorable being Sr.Fachtnan's 100th birthday, which we celebrated in the McAuley Home in Tralee a few days before I finished in Kinsale.

The involvement of the Sisters in the lives of the local people was something that I greatly admired. Sister Catherine knew everybody in the town and so many had been pupils of the Sisters in both schools.

During my time there six Sisters died and I found it a great privilege to be present at the bedside of these Sisters when they were dying; these were sacred moments.

Nobody could live in Kinsale and not be moved by the beauty of the place. I went for walks frequently around Compass Hill with its breath taking views over the Bandon Estuary, especially on a summer's evening when the sun was sinking behind the horizon. I enjoyed these walks and when I visit the Convent I always try to include a walk around the hill. I also loved the walks through the Convent fields with Sr.Colette who showed me every inch of the property, introducing me to hidden boreens and rights of way known by very few. The sense of history - both local and Mercy - is very strong in the Kinsale Community, and I was quickly introduced to names like Francis Bridgeman and Baptist Russell and their many foundations in Ireland, the States and England. I don't think anyone promoted Kinsale like Sr.Albert.

I enjoyed my years in Kinsale and this is evident from my frequent visits back since I left.

During my time there also the Convent's future was under discussion. This was a very difficult time for many Sisters. Change was inevitable, but it is my belief that it should be done with as little disturbance as possible especially to those who have spent all their lives in Kinsale Convent. In my opinion the Sisters' wishes are very important and whatever makes life easier or happier for them in the evening of their lives should be granted to them.

I still have very close contact with St.Joseph's School, as I am Chairperson of the Board of Management. The continuation of the Mercy ethos in the school is very important so I do all in my power to make sure that the good work done by the Mercy Sisters in Kinsale for education *continues into this new millennium.*

Another thing I liked was that I was frequently invited to celebrations and functions in the Town Hall and in this way I got to know a lot of the people in the town. The contact with the Friary I found very enriching and the weekly prayer group - Lectio Devina - gave me great spiritual enrichment".

Catherine Duggan from Macroom was a boarder at Our Lady of the Rosary School in the 1980's. Amid all the fun and frolic which must have endeared her to her fellow students and teachers is a true and lasting friend to the companions who lived these experiences with her.

"There were numerous fights to win the last piece of meringue on the refectory table and many stifled laughs as we glided downstairs at midnight for our "Midnight feast". Snorting with girlish laughter we would all hold our breaths in a 15 strong hush if we heard a nunnish creak or ancient door move. Then when we thought the shadowed coast was clear we would tiptoe the rest of the stairway to the senior study room to eat our "goodies", drink our watery lemonade and swap ghoulish outlandish stories.

As our giddiness crescendoed we moved our antics to a more upbeat activity - that of imitating our Sisters of Mercy. One or two mimics in the class would lay before our fresh imaginations a scenario of our Sisters involved in some dramatic fantasy or storyline; harmless and mildly forbidden fun on our part.

When I started in Boarding School as a naïve twelve-year-old I had no preconceived idea of what life would be like behind those grey walls. My subconscious illusion was of an Enid Blyton story with me playing a leading role. Reality was a tiny cubicle in a world removed from the security of home. We created our own security and fifteen twelve year olds grew up together. Friendships were formed and sealed very tightly, so bonded were those alliances for me that they have lasted through "thick and thin" and three of my closest friends emerged with me from my days in Kinsale.

I was prone and attracted to trouble and "high jinks". At the top of our first year dormitory Mother Baptist had a cubbyhole from her bedroom into the top cubicle facing down the dormitory, hence her eagle eye descended on every antic. Many nights she spied a flash of grey uniform dashing from one cubicle to the next as we made "French beds" for each other. Then she would suddenly appear and there would ensue a mad rush to hop into our respective beds, fully clothed. Needless to say we got entangled in sheets on our journey to slumberland due to "French bed syndrome"!

We led a relatively sheltered existence so occasionally girls of a more adventurous nature felt it necessary to sample local commercial life - namely sneak down town for a "gawk" around and top up on teenage treats. Ingenious excuses were invented as to why we had to leave the building! Once as a brazen fifteen year old I raced down town with my faithful Teddy under my arm, did nothing in particular, just enjoyed the glee of doing it, then nonchalantly rang the main doorbell to the Convent and when answered by a startled Sister, I related in graphic detail how "Teddy" had fallen out the window and had to be retrieved. Teddy to this day remains a silent witness to girlish escapades.

Many weathered excuses were proffered by young boarders and equally rejected by our wiser and oft weary superiors. When I and a fellow student on one occasion were caught with cigarettes I gallantly explained that they were a "present" for my father. Unfortunately my friend got reprimanded but I having Mafia type influence in the form of a great aunt in the very convent, namely, Sr.M.Oliver, got off lightly.

Once in Olympic type fashion I glided the length of a shiny corridor on a pillow in a pseudo sport we titled "pillow gliding". The corridor was of a highly polished consistency, so I failed to get an Olympic 9.9 when said pillow failed to stop at the very attractive stained glass door. The gliding pillow with me aboard having been pushed by lofty friends left a long crack in the door to starkly tell the tale.

There were many fun filled nights watching "Dallas" and "Top of the Pops" - two highlights in our weekly calendar. We would all sway back and forth to the music of Dallas and the catchy tunes of the '80's in the top 30.

Equally there were moments of homesickness and confinement, of food we did not care for and personality clashes that could not be avoided between ourselves and with our Sisters. But if you consider a couple of hundred women encased in the same environment for a long period of time you can conclude that we emerged with memories of humour and laughter, tears and sadness, anger and frustration; the mixed emotions of any given life really ...."

Mr Christie Fitzgerald of Butchers Row, now aged eighty-five, a former altar boy in the Parish Church remembers Quarant Ore - The Forty Hours - when Benediction was celebrated near the Rope Walk.

One hundred years after Catholic Emancipation, in 1929, the Eucharistic Procession was held in Kinsale for the first time finishing in the Convent Chapel where a lecture was given by Fr.Murphy C.C. Christy still remembers the text used on that occasion:

"It is strange but true that we are born away from our true home"

Later when he was sacristan at the Parish Church he recalls that because the nuns had to be in bed at nine o'clock he kept the habits for the dead - which were made in the Convent- in his own home. He was a considerate man, he did not wish to disturb the Sisters should there be a death during the night.

Mo Scéal Féin / My Own Story

I joined the Kinsale Community on October 31st 1965. I was surrounded by novices and dressed in the postulant's outfit - long black dress, stiff white collar and cuffs, and the bonnet. The "Bonnet," trial of anybody's vocation was a frilly halo surrounding the face with a bow tied under the chin and a piece of black net at the back and was worn until reception into the Order. It is not known who designed it!

Having tearfully parted with my family, I accompanied the other novices into supper and there for the first time I realised the size of the Community. It was an extraordinary experience. Being Halloween there were apples, nuts, ginger biscuits and barm brack. I sat at the end of the novices' table in a state of bewilderment. I had never seen so much black and white, or heard such banging and clanging of crockery; there must have been over fifty Sisters in the refectory. I had not been to boarding school so I found this experience of Communal eating strange. The Refectory was set out rather like it would be for a wedding - a top table accommodating the Rev.Mother Imelda, Mother Enda Assistant Rev.Mother, Mother Emmanuel Bursar, and Mother Oliver the Novice Mistress. The other tables came down on either side with the Sisters seated in order of seniority. The novices, about twelve of us, sat at the end of a long table under the keen eye of Mother Oliver. Poor woman, she turned various shades of puce as her charges laughed too loudly, overfilled their mouths, had their elbows on the table or looked around too much - taking each of these transgressions in decorum personally. There was a great empty space in the middle of the floor for the servers to move about freely. After supper we were allowed watch television for an hour. This was a special concession for the novices, as the reopening of the Cork Opera House was being shown.

The bell rang for night prayer at nine o'clock. This marked the beginning of The Great Silence which would continue until after breakfast the following morning. As new recruits -there were three of us - we were exempt from spiritual exercises for the first week in order to become familiar with our surroundings. This week I feel was a bit of a waste as we would have been able to appreciate it better after a few months when we were more settled. On that first night while the community were saying Compline we were shepherded to the organ gallery for a brief prayer by Sr.Mary (O'Donoghue) our senior by four months. We followed her around for a whole week. It must have been a funny sight as she was quite tall and the three of us postulants were all short, it was rather like a mother hen and her chicks!

Nazareth, sited under the noviceship which is now the Prayer Room, was the sleeping quarter for the novices. It was a very compact wing away from the rest of the house.

On that first night I found it a terrifying place. The heavy shutters on my window were shut and bolted, the room was Spartan and the main light switch was turned off at ten o'clock. If there was any way I could have escaped I would have and run away as far as possible. Between loneliness and the utter starkness of my surroundings I forgot about my religious vocation and the major step towards saving the world which I had taken on that day!

Within about two weeks I had started to settle down and grow accustomed to my surroundings, when Sr.Kathleen Costin one of my companions died. This was a difficult time for the whole Community but more especially for those of us who lived in Nazareth with her. We were terrified and used to huddle together in one or other cell for some time afterwards. Mother Oliver was so kind; she accompanied us each night and patrolled Nazareth until she thought we were all asleep.

When the rising bell rang at six o'clock each morning it felt like the middle of the night to me, as bleary eyed I made my way to the choir for Morning Prayer and Meditation followed by the Community Mass at seven thirty.

Once I had recovered from my dreadful loneliness and Sr.Kathleen's death I enjoyed my time as a postulant. I even coped with the Rising Bell. St. Therese of Lisieux is supposed to have said that we are as pleasing to the Lord asleep as awake. I do hope this is true as I slept my way through Meditation many a morning!

The eight months as a postulant passed quickly. I learned about the various works of the Congregation, visited the sick and elderly and had the opportunity to work in both the Primary and Secondary Schools. I learned the various prayer forms and hours. In those days we recited the Little Office of the Blessed Virgin in Latin. Latin is a wonderful prayer language – it transcends the ordinary daily events and takes us to a different place.

I was received into the Mercy Congregation in June 1966. At the clothing ceremony I received the habit, the veil and the choir cloak. It has always been a private ceremony in the Mercy Congregation, and I remember it as a simple but beautifully symbolic event. During the Canonical or Spiritual year which followed Reception I studied the Rule, Canon Law and delved deeply into the Scriptures. Life was simple, I did as I was told (most of the time) and had no responsibility. My companions in the Noviceship were a wonderful group of people, all very creative, bright and full of fun. It was a happy time and I have maintained a close relationship with all those with whom I shared this experience.

As a second year white veil I had some study time and I worked in the schools, teaching Drama and Elocution as well as Religious Education, typing and Civics. It was a busy time entering students for drama, public speaking debating competitions, and also elocution examinations.

During my time in the Convent, I had many house duties. Each Sister was allocated a house duty, being responsible for the cleanliness and smooth running of a section of the convent. This was a very good system; straight after breakfast each Sister attended to her duty thus ensuring that the building was ship-shape before the school day began. I worked in the Sacristy for a while. This was a busy assignment, particularly in the summer when as many as eight or nine priests would come to say a "private" Mass in Latin. These were the days before Concelebration. There were often three Masses going on at once, which we as novices had to serve.

Assistant to Sr.Raphael, the Sister in charge of the Community Room was another post I held. I loved working with the indomitable Sr.Raphael. She and I came from the same neck of the woods, and we had many a good laugh together. Over the years I was responsible for various lengths of corridors, toilets, bathrooms and stairways, but my last assignment was the Infirmary, which I disliked intensely - God never intended me to be a nurse. Nursing, I believe to be a high and noble vocation not within my grasp. Visiting the sick and doing little services like fetching a drink or a book from the library is within my limits but I've not got the stomach for any more. Fortunately there was no real bout of illness during my Infirmary days!

At the end of two years as a white veil I made my first profession. Many of my companions were heading off to college; my superiors didn't appear to know what to do with me! I had entered with a fairly good leaving certificate and had matriculated so I failed to see what the problem was - not that it was much of a problem to me at the time. I was quite content pursuing my various activities mentioned previously, working with great teachers and convinced of my own sanctity and importance in the scheme of things, doing God's will while my contemporaries "in the world" were indulging themselves in all sorts of selfish ways!

They say that "Pride comes before a fall;" well I was soon to be shaken out of my complacency. I suppose I grew up and suddenly began to see things in their true light and to question the system. The Noviceship was beginning to split up with people going to college and after yearly professions joining the large Community and I, of course, was the last novice until Sr.Mairead Healy arrived almost ten years later.

Life in the Noviceship was very sheltered. Mother Oliver, the Novice mistress, while strict and austere, was wonderfully kind. She protected us in a way that a mother hen would protect her chicks, she saw to it that we all had the benefit of a third level education, as well as opportunities to learn music, singing and elocution while in her care.

After much discussion it was decided that I should be trained as a Primary School teacher in England; I actually enjoyed working with older children and would have preferred to have gone to University. I felt somewhat like a parcel as I set off from Dublin Airport for Newcastle upon Tyne to a teacher training college run by the Sacred Heart Sisters. Sadly this college no longer exists, but it was thriving in 1969. I had scarcely been outside the Convent walls since I entered and here I was heading for another country. When I arrived it was like being on another planet. Fortunately I met Sr.Bosco Cogger, a Sister of Mercy from Mayo, on the 'plane and she felt just as strange as I did. We became firm friends that day and have remained so ever since. My main subject was to be drama with subsidiary dance, subjects no nun had ever before taken at this particular college. I thanked God for Sr.Catriona Dilworth, a Sister of Mercy from Ballyshannon, who was taking main course P.E. We were a great consolation to each other. Can you imagine prancing about a stage in a religious habit?... Or doing the various warm-up and improvisation activities on the floor? Well drama is a subject pursued by few; we were fifteen in my year group. Special permission was secured for me to wear clothes suitable to my dramatic pursuits - jeans, t-shirts, leotards and such like. The other students eyed me with suspicion to start with, but soon we had built up a trust and I got on famously with them. The initial difficulty of the course was that I was totally out of touch with what was going on in the world of drama and television, particularly in the U.K. as we did not have access to the BBC in those days. I had never heard of Morecombe and Wise, or Dixon of Dock Green, or even Coronation Street. I knew nothing about English football, but I soon learned and in no time I was "Manager" of the Drama Society Football team, which was indeed an honour. We won the championship one year and when I left college the Captain, Roy Stanley, presented me with his medal which is still one of my most prized possessions.

The Sacred Heart Sisters were women of great vision. They had opened up to the changes that were happening in Religious life. Almost over night they had changed from a semi-enclosed order to being actively involved in the community and wearing ordinary clothes. There was a great openness to the Spirit and people came to realise their personal worth. They, of course, had a great influence on those of us who were student nuns at the time. During my college years I learned a lot about life and about myself; I saw the relevance of religious life and my own place in it. They were fruitful and full years and I thoroughly enjoyed them.

In the second year of my course, I made my final profession - that lifelong commitment to the Mercy way of life. That is a very big step and should never happen amid the distractions of college life - now, of course it does not. I believed in the future; I had seen the changes which had taken place within other Congregations and knew that these changes were inevitable, which is why I read my vows with confidence.

With my family on my profession day.

When I left college in 1973 and returned to Kinsale, it was rather like stepping back in time. I know that the institution does not change as quickly as the individual, but I had experienced the Religious life lived in the twentieth century. Vatican 11 had clearly defined the role of the Sister, and I felt that Sisters of Mercy over and above any other order must be women of their time, as Catherine McAuley was. Sadly I left Kinsale in 1974 knowing very little about this wonderful woman who has been such an inspiration to me since.

Back in 1973 some of the rules and regulations appeared to be more important than the Spirit of the Foundress. This was a time of great change: age old ways of life were being questioned; people who had lived in a particular way for thirty, forty or even fifty years were being asked to change, to accept new ideas, new ways of thinking. Change is painful, and the older one gets the more painful it is. When I entered the convent at the age of eighteen my superiors were in their sixties or seventies. We had left totally different worlds. How could they be expected to be aware of the difficulties of a world that they had been out of touch with for so long? Nuns stayed in their convents unless it was necessary for them to visit the sick or the poor, and then they travelled out in twos with eyes downcast, without speaking to anybody until they reached their destination. This was never the intention of Catherine McAuley.

The Catholic Church as a whole was in turmoil in the seventies; there was a tug of war between the old and the young, the former trying to do "what was always done," the young looking for challenge and a channel for their boundless energy. A psychologist would probably say that the needs of the young were not being met - think of Mother Baptist Russell, aged twenty-five, setting off on an amazing adventure! Life is either an amazing adventure or it is nothing.

It was a sad state of affairs but I can honestly say people on all sides acted from purely honourable motives. People believed that they were doing God's will as they saw it.

My mother died shortly after I left college, and I shall never forget the kindness I received from my fellow-sisters at the time. They would sit with me late into the night when for several months I was unable to sleep. Sr.Immaculata, acting Rev.Mother, at the time, was particularly kind and supportive; she did not say a lot - she is not a very talkative woman- but she has a charisma. In those early weeks and months after the funeral she would just look at me and smile this beatific smile which let me know she understood the pain.

I taught a Senior Infants Class - beautiful children whom I really enjoyed teaching. When the Infants went home at two thirty, I taught dance to the other classes in the Primary School. This was great because the older children seemed to be so creative. After school I worked with Vera Herlihy; we had a lovely group of girls for drama and dance. I have worked in many schools since and taught many children, but working with my colleagues and young people in Kinsale was a very precious time, and no other school or children have captured my heart in quite the same way.

Pictured with one of my students Daniel O'Sullivan on his First Holy Communion Day.

The Late Father Brian Kelly

My good friend, the late Fr.Brian Kelly, was a curate in Kinsale during my days there. We shared a love of drama and literature. He was a terrific support in all the ventures undertaken in the schools. He was always actively involved in the activities of the students and no doubt many of them remember him with great affection as I do.

At that time I felt a great need to take responsibility for my own life. The convent, which during the noviceship had been rather like a nest -a safe place -, had now become a cage, restricting my need to fly.

Eventually I applied to Rome and asked to be dispensed from my vows. The dispensation arrived on December 14th 1974 I was quite prepared to wait until the end of term before leaving, but things were such at the time that I had to go to the Bishop's house on that day to sign the dispensation and leave from there. The overwhelming feeling of that period was one of great sadness.

I have no regrets. When I entered the Convent in 1965 that was the beginning of my spiritual journey. My journey took me away from Kinsale physically, but I have retained a close association with the Convent and the Sisters I have known and loved there, many now dead.

I remember with great affection the gentle Sr.Angela who fed so many people. She was the first point of contact for any visitor arriving at the convent and what a shining example of Mercy hospitality she was. Sr.Albert returned from Florida to become bursar to the community. She was a gracious lady who never missed an opportunity of doing a kindness. Sr.Michael was a very old nun when I entered and I remember her regularly saying, "May you never get arthritis." Many of the Sisters worked so very hard, I remember Sr.Columba on the farm, Sr.Virgilius caring for the plants and the garden even though her health was not good. Sr.Cecilia worked in the laundry, another humble soul. Sr.Evangelist was head infirmarian when I was a novice. She was another independent thinker. Sr.Lawrence was always smiling and ready for a chat, in spite of being profoundly deaf. Since amalgamation many new Sisters have come to Kinsale and many of those I lived with have gone to other convents in the Cork area. But no matter where we go we are all part of the Mercy family.

Being a Sister of Mercy was an enriching experience, one I shall always treasure. I have treated the convent as home since my own home was sold over twenty years ago. My husband, my son and myself have always received a warm welcome over the years, and nobody has more "aunties" nuns than my son Neil.

I share the Community's grief at the closure of St.Joseph's and my prayer is that the Sisters will continue their wonderful Mercy hospitality and have many happy years in their new home in Winters Hill.

Chapter 7
Future Hopes.

A Religious Vocation is a call to contemplation, a call to closer union with God. I do not know of any Sister, Priest or Brother who entered religious life because they wanted to teach, nurse or engage in social work.

Father Laurence Freeman, a Benedictine Monk and Director of the Christian Meditation movement revived over twenty years ago by his fellow Benedictine - Father John Main -, calls the worldwide community of Christian meditators the "Monastery without Walls". This is very significant, as nowadays so many people who have given up attending their Churches are daily meditators. Ireland's First Lady - President Mary McAleese, is a fine example of a busy lady fitting meditation into her daily life. She led The John Main Seminar in Dublin in 1997, before she became President! Other leaders have been such spiritual giants as The Dalai Lama, Bede Griffiths, Jean Vanier, Robert Kiely, Thomas Keating and several other well-known thinkers in the field of spirituality. The whole of the 1997 Conference is documented in President Mary's book "Reconciled Being" which is well worth reading. Meditation is a unifying form of prayer where people of all religious persuasions and none can come together in the silence. Since the days of the Desert Ammas and Abbas, meditation has been in our Christian Tradition but it unfortunately fell into disuse until John Main revived it. He made it his life's work to bring meditative prayer into the mainstream of Christian experience. Thankfully his work continues to grow.

Sister Agnes Beary runs a Christian Meditation group in Kinsale, where she is also providing a valuable service at "The Healing Centre". Here she explains why she became interested in complementary therapies and healing.

"As a child I used to help my father and grandfather to collect and prepare herbs. They used them to treat sick animals on the farm, and my grandmother prepared them to give to people who were ill. I have very vivid memories of people coming to my home asking for these remedies and returning after some time to proclaim that they had worked wonders for them. Actually when I finished school I had the idea that I would study these remedies, but at the time there were great medical advances in the Western World and the interest in complementary therapies began to wane, so I left my boats behind me and entered Kinsale.

The years I spent working in Kenya stimulated my interest once more in natural therapies. The natives there are very wedded to these remedies, but occasionally use them without discretion. I have disturbing memories of some poor women being brought to the hospital in obstructed labour, having been treated by the witch doctor for several days in the Bush. On arrival in the

Maternity Unit they were completely exsanguinated and died in a few hours. I also have very happy memories of Kenya. I delivered hundreds of babies and the mothers were so grateful for the help that they christened the girls "Sister Agnes" in addition to the tribal name. Hopefully when I reach the "Pearly Gates" there will be lots of "Sr.Agnes" to welcome me Home!

While working as a Tutor in St.Finbarr's Hospital, in my spare time I began to study some of these remedies to find out what they had to offer to people. Reflextherapy, Aromatherapy, Therapeutic Healing, Bio-Testing Therapy, Magnet Therapy, Geopathic and Personal Stress were amongst those I studied, and I also gained Certification in Counselling Techniques.

In August 1993 with the kind permission of Sister Imelda O'Shaughnessy, Mother General, I opened a Healing Centre in my beloved Kinsale. It was my earnest wish to walk in the footsteps of Mother Francis Bridgeman, who left the Convent in Kinsale to go to the Crimean War and heal the soldiers in the trenches and hospitals there. Had I been in Kinsale then I would have accompanied her on the journey - wishful thinking!

The Healing Centre has stimulated an enormous interest - more than I could have ever dreamed of. I feel so happy that I can help so many people from all walks of life. Some people who come are suffering from psychological and emotional trauma and just need a listening ear and a shoulder to cry on. It amazes me the reverence, respect and trust which these people have for nuns, and of course I was no stranger to them as I worked in the local hospital for many years.

If the occasion arises that people are confined to their homes I treat them there. If I have time to spare I go to the Hospice in Cork and treat patients who are terminally ill. This I find very rewarding: I feel the Lord is using me to heal these people - what an awe-inspiring thought! I feel totally unworthy.

It can all be summed up in a statement made by a client whom I had treated - "I feel mighty". What more could I ask for as a Sister of Mercy?"

Sr. Agnes Beary in her Healing clinic.

I feel we are in the midst of a great paradigm shift, something new and wonderful is being birthed. Our Universe has evolved in a blessed way, the conditions needed for life appearing just when needed and so has been the story of our human evolution. The great Congregations of Religious appeared as they were needed in the world. Now the needs which they were founded to meet are being met largely by State bodies, thus freeing the Sisters to move again to the margins and meet the evolving needs of our time. I do not feel religious were ever meant to be in the "mainstream" of Church life but on the margins, at the coal face where the poor (not necessarily the materially poor) and needy are to be found.

The great need of today's world is a spiritual one, which is clearly not being met by the Churches. As we move from Duality (either or) to Nonduality (both and) we see how the connectedness and the oneness of all creation makes the divisions between religions inappropriate. As we move beyond ideologies into deep ecumenism it is important that we honour the Divine in all of life. The great twentieth century monk and mystic, Dom Bede Griffiths, who went to India in 1956 "to find the other half of his soul" says that religious differences are purely cultural. He likens them to the fingers of the hand which are separate, but as you move down they become one at the palm. Bede of course was echoing the words of the great medieval mystic, Meister Eckhart, who says, "God is a great underground river that no one can dam up and no one can stop", and from whom we all draw our strength. No matter what religion we belong to the fundamental message is the same - Unconditional Love - being able to reach out in compassion as Mercy Sisters have been doing since 1831. We have read in Chapter Three that the pioneering Sisters did not ask what the religion of the suffering person was, they just got on and ministered to them.

Mercy Sisters, I know are working with the homeless, with refugees and with asylum seekers. This is an appropriate ministry for us Irish, when as recent as a century ago so many of our people had to flee from the famine and disease which was raging in our country. Life was sad and difficult for those asylum seekers trying to eke out a living in a foreign shore where they were often badly treated and given the poorest housing and most menial jobs. We know that it took a generation for them to integrate in their new communities and go on to become people of whom we can be justly proud. Today's marginalised must feel the same pain and inadequacy, and it is right and proper that we reach out in compassion and love, and help them rebuild their lives in what is to them a foreign land.

It is prudent to plan for the future but living in the now is more important, knowing that this is the only moment we have got. Yesterday is history and tomorrow is a blank page; we need to be mindful of the immediate needs of all beings.

Sister Josephine who joined the Kinsale Community in 1989 and who has first hand experience of working with the marginalised has this to say:

"I became a member of the Kinsale Mercy Community nearly twelve years ago. Having spent one year teaching in the school I was asked to return to Peru, where I have been ministering in a poor barrio for almost eleven years. I feel privileged to have had the Kinsale Community as my base where I was welcomed and supported with the usual Mercy hospitality. Surrounded by the natural scenic beauty of Kinsale one is constantly reminded of the Great Artist and Creator who is our God.

The history associated with the town and the Mercy Community (documented already here) is a valuable heritage as we now live in this post-modern Ireland.

Life today is very different from past years: The Sisters of Mercy are fewer in number and may wear a different garb, but the Mercy Charism lives on. The cry of the poor and marginalised is still being heard in Kinsale where frequently many non governmental organisations and volunteers come together to respond to the needs of the old, the destitute and the exploited, at home and in the Third World Countries e.g. Romania, Chernobyl, Peru, the Philippines, to name a few. The solidarity of the local community is to be admired. Our Foundress Catherine McAuley, would say that no poor person should go away empty handed, and certainly in Kinsale no appeal goes unheard. The Liberation Theologian, Gustavo Gutierrez, tells us that the "preferential option for the poor" should not be just for priests and religious, but the decision of every Christian. My hope is that the younger generation, who have never known poverty in Ireland, can inherit what has so wonderfully characterised their parents and local communities and live out that option in their own culture.

As the Sisters will no longer live in the present Convent it is important that it should take its place among the many other memorials of the past in Kinsale, as a symbol of the Mercy and Service to a poorer Ireland and to many countries abroad. This would still serve to inspire us all to continue the great tradition with the enthusiasm and vitality that empowered our Mercy Sisters of the past. It would also greatly enhance the touristic attractions of Kinsale.

When asked to have input in this work, one of the points for consideration was: "The Way Forward" I can only give my own thoughts. While recognising our contribution to the Church and to society and maintaining our roots in the past, we need to hear the challenges of the present age, as members of the Church. The Congregation may decline and even cease to be but our membership is primarily of the Universal Roman Catholic Church, and it is in this context that building The Kingdom of God here takes place.

In my work in Peru I experienced a much more alive and participative Church in which the laity could truly feel it was really their Church. For me this was a very enriching experience. The absence of this is a great loss both to the official Church and to the members. We need to connect much more with the laity than we have done heretofore. We need their valuable contribution of potential and service, not just as substitutes for the shortage of priests or religious but in their own right in many areas such as - faith, spirituality, culture and insertion in the secular world. With the affluence and rapid technological changes Ireland is no longer the Island of Saints and Scholars. Nevertheless there are very many good people concerned about injustices, violence, oppression, corruption, abortion, addiction, immorality and indifference so common in our country. Have we solicited their help or advice? Even with a good economy, are people happy? Could it be that we are living in the midst of people and not knowing what's going on in their lives? Are we so busy with our own little projects that we have no time to investigate the real world at home, not to mention the larger world? Do we know there is also a world outside the EU which we are exploiting every day? Why not ask people what they know? It is still a very unfinished business and we each have made a commitment as a Christian that perhaps we no longer remember."

Sister Catherine Linehan is well known in Kinsale, where she goes about "doing good". She lobbies Councillors to get housing for older people and will not take "no" for an answer until her beloved ladies or gentlemen are happily installed in suitable accommodation. The town honoured her with "A Local Achievements Award" for her services to the local community and chose her as Grand Marshall leading the St.Patrick's Day parade in 2000.

The Guardwell Sheltered Housing Scheme, the brainchild of Heidi Roche, is a facility of which Kinsale can be proud. It consists of sixteen units in an aesthetically pleasing site. The residents live independently but have the use of a recreation room where they can gather to meet and chat. Sr.Benignus, retired from the Sacred Heart Hospital, lives in an apartment in the complex and is available to the residents of this centre should they need nursing care or help.

Sr.Kevin O'Brien feels that the future now is in the hands of the laity.

"Since our numbers are decreasing and the majority of our Sisters are advancing in age and hopefully in wisdom and grace, the presence of the Sisters in the local community through a "chat" a "visit" or a "smile", and of course through the prayers of those who are housebound, to me is a huge ministry in today's world. The "being", not "doing", is important now. The presence of the Sisters has contributed enormously in the teaching and nursing fields, and our schools and hospital are in the hands of excellent people with a true Mercy ethos.

Perhaps we could collaborate with the laity, enabling people to get involved in Parish activities, by perhaps funding them through training courses, etc."

Sr.Elma Coakley introduced the weeks of guided prayer into Kinsale. These were held in the school every Lent for the people of the Parish. This and Spiritual Direction are important ministries which Sisters of Mercy are involved in throughout the world. Here are Sr.Elma's thoughts on this ministry.

"I think prayer ministry and spirituality is very important and should be a big part of Mercy in today's society - answer to spiritual hunger.

Regarding homelessness, substance abuse, etc. I think now that we are a wealthy country with our own government, the state should take responsibility for these issues."

Sister (Professor) Eleanor O'Leary has worked in UCC full time since 1981. She is highly committed to life in UCC having been elected by the graduates to the Governing Body on four occasions. She has worked mainly with disability equality, ageism and staff-student relationships on this Board. The Students Union of UCC presented her with a Special Award for her service to students (the first time such an Award was presented to a Governor of UCC). She was the first female Head of the Department of Applied Psychology during 2000 - 2001; particularly apt in her case, as she believes passionately in the equality of women. She has been Director of the Counselling and Health Studies Unit since 1984. Her colleagues in the Psychological Society of Ireland awarded her the special award for outstanding contribution to psychology in 2000.

Sr.Eleanor comments on her ministry within third level education in the Dept. of Applied Psychology, University College Cork, and the future.

"My ministry is a different but much loved one - so loved that someone could validly criticise me for overworking. However, I grew in a novitiate where the words of St.Ignatius rang in my ears "Laborare est Orare" - To work is to pray.

Sisters of Mercy will, I believe, continue to create new furrows as long as the Congregation exists. Catherine McAuley's work focused on empowerment and faith and these continue to be our foci as Mercy Sisters.

My work relates particularly to the former. As a counsellor educator, I was privileged to educate around one hundred school counsellors from 1981 to 1991. During this time, my first two books `The Psychology of Counselling`(Cork University Press 1982) and `The Challenge of 2001`(Cork: Tower Press 1987) were published. The latter was a social and psychological analysis of the parishes which the Mercy Sisters in Cork and Ross worked. Fr.Brian Kelly, my mentor and friend served as advisor to the work.

The emphasis in my work is on personal growth, the ability of individuals to grow and develop emotionally, socially and spiritually up to the moment of death. My book `Gestalt Therapy: Theory, Research and Practice`(Cork University Press 1992), is devoted to facilitating this personal growth. I believe that it is one of the best ways I can contribute to the quality of life of human beings. The core of the nine courses in counselling, psychotherapy and personal development which I pioneered in UCC have this particular emphasis. I believe that the fullness of life is found in being human and holy. Too often in the past in religious life, these two dimensions were viewed as mutually exclusive.

In the last twelve months, my research on homelessness in UCC entitled 'The Southern Homeless Project' was funded by the Order. The team in the Counselling and Health Studies Unit (Kathleen O'Sullivan, David O'Sullivan and Jonathan Gallagher) interviewed 171 homeless adults who were over 18 years, in Counties Cork, Waterford, Wexford and Kilkenny. The causes of homelessness together with the lifestyle, risk factors and time structure of homeless individuals were investigated.

Marginalised individuals in general, are the foci of my research work with my major interest being older adults. I publish as much as possible on the subject knowing that my audience is an international one and hoping that our publications from the Unit are helping the quality of life of marginalised individuals. Ageism is still rife in Ireland and much work needs to be done on it. My book, 'Counselling Older Adults' (Chapman & Hall, 1996) devotes a full chapter to the subject. Inge Nieuwstraten has assisted me in investigating and writing on older people in nursing homes. Since 1993, an important dimension of this work has been the weekly visits of graduate students under my supervision to older people in Cuskinny Court. Counselling groups and individual counselling are offered to those who want to avail of it. The owners, Catriona and Victor O'Flynn, have spared no effort to enhance the quality of life of the older people residing there, while the older people themselves have taken great pride in assisting us with our research. This reciprocity is a very essential part of the work.

A development of which I am particularly proud is the training of counsellors in Keyna, since 1993. From its inception Kevin O'Connor has worked with me on this project. Sr.Leonie Boland, a Mercy Sister attached to the Amari Centre, Nairobi, approached me as to the possibility of UCC offering a qualification in counselling to Keynan and Tanzanian students. No sooner said than done when two Mercy Sisters are involved! It is a joy for me in 2001 to know that professional counselling has been established in Kenya and that our former students and Diplomates have been to the forefront in this development. A member of the Unit, Deirdre O'Shea, left home and family and traveled to Kenya to teach group facilitation skills. A special thanks to Kevin and Deirdre for their dedication to the education of Kenyan counsellors.

This year, I was asked to be responsible for the support and counselling of non EU students on campus so this new academic year will bring new experiences. This, I feel, is at the heart of Mercy - adjusting and responding to circumstances as they emerge. Being an active rather than a contemplative religious, this involvement in action outcomes, development, *empowerment and marginalisation will continue to be part of the Mercy Charism for as long as God wants Sisters of Mercy in this world. May He inspire other young women to continue the work."*

The peace and tranquility of the Chapel and Choir at St.Joseph's Convent have been commented on already. The whole ethos of Mercy Convent Kinsale is one of prayer and silence. Like many Convents at the present time, it is providing a space where a silent and prayerful atmosphere prevails, and where people can come to be nourished and reach that still quiet place within them, which is of course God. Living in awareness of the Divine dwelling in each being does, I feel, change our attitudes to all of life, challenging us to treat all with the respect which is their due as sparks of the Divine - daughters and sons of God. I read recently in an inspirational book by Paramahansa Yogananda, the man who introduced the practice of yoga to the West: "A diamond is still a diamond even if it is covered with mud". This certainly would affect our relationship with all of our broken humanity. In a sensitive and nonjudgmental way the Sisters of Mercy care for people broken by substance abuse and by drug and alcohol addiction, and people affected by the aids virus.

Since I reconnected with my wonderful Celtic Spiritual Tradition I have started leading workshops to celebrate the Celtic Festivals. During the past three years Sisters and former Sisters from Kinsale have joined me in Inchadoheny, Co. Cork to celebrate Samhain and to appreciate in a creative way the many blessings which the universe daily bestows on us and to connect with our Celtic ancestors - The Communion of Saints. The Celtic tradition is rich in Kinsale, in the persons of the older Sisters and townspeople who have a prayer for every occasion, in the peaceful grounds with the Celtic Crosses marking the resting places of generations of Sisters, and in the beauty of the town and its surroundings. It is easy to take our pain to the sea or the mountains, which have an extraordinarily healing effect. Engaging with our fellow beings and knowing that they also have a purpose just as we have might alter our perspective and halt our greed. We may begin to be protective of species, which are dying at the rate of one every twenty-five minutes. In our present world the greatest need is to "live lightly" on our planet home, a home of such extraordinary beauty that it turned many of the astronauts who saw it from space into mystics. Our "primitive" ancestors knew that we lived on a living-breathing planet; they never saw the Creator as separate from or outside creation, thankfully now we are rediscovering this truth. Our scientists and theologians are no longer in dispute; many are working together for the good of the whole, Albert Einstein has said, "Science without religion is lame. Religion without science is blind".

My dream is, that at some future time the Sisters of Mercy will initiate a project for the use of some of their land in Kinsale for the purpose of developing a "Shared Earth" project. Some Sisters in Rosscarbery (who also belong to the Southern Province of the Congregation) have taken up this important issue already. They are experimenting with projects, which will raise all our awareness to the need for honouring and celebrating our planet home in an appropriate way, and stop the mindless vandalism in which we have previously engaged. An elder statesman of this important work, Thomas Berry, a Passionist priest now in his eighties, considers the earth as primary. He says: "Unless we are totally depraved we will seek to give to our children not only life and education but a planet with pure air and bright waters and fruitful fields, a planet that can be lived on with grace and beauty and a touch of human and earthly tenderness." He also says: "All human institutions, programmes, policies and decisions must be judged primarily by the extent to which they inhibit, ignore, or foster a mutually dependent human-earth relationship."

Father Berry was a disciple of Teilhard de Chardin, the French Jesuit who was silenced by the Catholic Church for teaching what today is accepted by all those who are at the cutting edge of theology and science.

It is gratifying to know that Catherines McAuley's vision is still being lived by the great Mercy family, consisting of so many ordinary women and men who are engaged in the foregoing activities. It must make her heart sing with "the holy excitement" she so often talked about when the poor were being served.

The world will always need those who are prepared to go the extra mile for peace and justice for all beings by lobbying governments on their behalf, writing letters, being at the heart of decision making and remaining always vigilant that those in need are served. This is why I feel confident that Mercy will continue in Kinsale with the love and support of the local community of which the Sisters are an integral part. With confidence I echo the words of Julian of Norwich the fourteenth century English Mystic that:

"All will be well,

and all will be well

and every manner of thing will be well."

Chapter 8
Cherished Memories

I leave the last word to Sister Immaculata Hourihane, one of the most senior Sisters of the Community, who has so lovingly encapsulated the Mercy Story in Kinsale.

Dear Mothers Francis and Mary Anne
And all the dear sisters.

I write this long letter

To you we love so dear,

To thank you for your kindness

And to beg of you draw near.

We know you loved this Convent

And tended it with care,

But alas, its days are ended,

Now people stand and stare.

You strove to make it worthy

Of our Lord and King,

Where the sisters all together

His praises there could sing.

To day we're sad and lonely,

With darkness closing in;

'St.Joseph's' is no longer Home,

Some say, "it is a sin".

We'd like to reminisce with you

On times now far away,

When the future did seem bright

As the blossoms of the May.

Mercy in Kinsale

Come, we'll take you for a visit

To a famed and ancient spot.

It's the oldest town in Ireland,

And that's saying quite a lot.

Yes, I know that you remember;

It's the old town of Kinsale,

Where on its lovely harbour

The tourists love to sail.

Within this tranquil haven
Stood a stately Convent tall,
Like a beacon in the darkness
Shedding light to one and all.

In the hallowed chapel
The sisters met each day,
To render God due homage
And to plead for all who stray.

It was a place of learning,
And a powerhouse of true prayer.
The orphan, poor and lonely,
Always found a refuge there.

In famine, war or sickness
The nuns were always there,
Rendering their assistance
With tender loving care.

We recall the workroom
And the famous "Kinsale Lace".
At home, abroad, in every land,
It took pride of place.

Kinsale was not found wanting

Whenever there was need.

We tried to build God's Kingdom

`By prayer and work and deed.

Hence, it's many great foundations

Carrying Catherine's banner wide.

We bravely faced the dangers,

The Holy Spirit was our Guide.

Receptions and Professions

Were special days apart;

And the Jubilee celebrations,

In which all of us took part.

We remember Quarant Ore

With the choirs that sang so well,

And all the plays and concerts

With much, much more to tell.

Continuity

Education's still our mission,

Social Work and Healthcare too.

We want labourers for the vineyard

To share in what we do.

Since our work is not completed

We strive anew each day,

To bear witness to Christ's presence

And lead souls along "His Way".

We pray, O Virgin Mother,

Help us to always be

Channels of God's mercy,

Setting all His children free.

In Kinsale's long, long history

It has weathered many a storm;

When it came to our "Good Friday"

We looked for "Easter Morn".

Interior of Convent:

In the front and back parlours
Is where our history began,
And continued thro' the decades
Like the melody of song.

The community room was lovely,
The parlours, choir and hall;
But the little convent chapel
Was the loveliest gem of all.

The beautiful winding staircase,
Our pride and our delight,
The ascending steps so gentle,
That we noticed, not its height.

The corridors were spacious,
The windows large and tall,
Letting in God's sunshine;
There were rooms for all.

Think of "Nazareth" and the "Prayer Room,"
And the memories rush in.
There we began our noviceship,
Gaining solace from within.

With so many saints to guard us,
How could we go astray?
And the scriptural scrolls to guide us
And help us on our way.

The furniture and silver,
And the artifacts of old,
What belonged to our loved Foundress,
We must cherish, care, and hold.

The Apostles' Corridor
Was different from the rest.
'Twas there the founding sisters
First lived and took their rest.

It was later the Infirmary,
Yet the sick were not alone.
See the room where Mass was offered
When on their journey home.

The ground floor of the Convent
Looked very like the past,
With its quaint old tiling
That was surely meant to last.

How many times we saw you
Climb the Back Stairs,
It was near the Infirmary
And linked to former days.

The kitchen was important.
It was airy, it was bright.
There was cooked the tasty food
That was savoured with delight.

Close by was the Refectory
Where we had our meals in peace.
In its relaxing atmosphere
We truly felt at ease.

Every inch of the building
Had a special tale to tell;
And all so very interesting,
'Twas a lovely place to dwell.

The Exterior - Back:

See the old flag passage,

With St.Michael's hand raised high

To protect the Blessed Sacrament

And the grounds and buildings nigh.

The garden was so peaceful,

And the paths we walked each day;

The graves where you lie sleeping

To await the "Final Day".

Each summer on the balcony

We spent times of bliss.

O, the joy and peace and happiness

We now so sadly miss.

There is still the playground

Where the junior children play.

It is an apt reminder

Of a bygone day.

Hear the animals on the farm,

See the apples on the trees,

Taste the fruits and vegetables

And the honey from the bees.

Who could forget the "Rope Walk"

Or the tennis courts nearby?

Remembering all the beauty

We heave a heartfelt sigh.

Exterior - Front:

Look at that great convent,

Watch God's plan for it unfold,

Its contribution to the Order

When all its history's told.

The Front door was a symbol

Of the Holy Door,

Reminding all who entered

That Jesus said, "I am the Door".

It was also historic,

For through it the sisters went:

Those going on new foundations,

And willingly they went.

At Christ's second coming

All things will be new,

Then the convent that we loved so well

Will wear a fragrant hue.

Heavenly Companionship:

Draw near to us, dear sisters,

For the night is dark and drear,

Keep our eyes on Lumen Christi

And drive away all fear.

We think that we should see you,

Feel the touch of each dear hand,

Hear you softly whisper:

"We're in the Promised Land.

For we on earth hath union

With God the three in one,

And Mystic Sweet Communion

With those whose rest is won."

You were contemplatives in action

Through your Mercy way of life.

You learned to be one with God

Amid the din and strife.

Let us ask our Blessed Mother

With St.Joseph, our true friend,

And Father McNamara

To befriend us to the end.

We thank you most sincerely

For your heritage so rare,

And the home we loved so dearly,

St.Joseph's convent fair.

To God be all the Glory

For His many gifts sublime,

And He promised to be with us

'Til the very end of time.

Some day we hope to join you

With the Holy ones and blest,

And the Company of Angel hosts,

In God we find our rest.

Le grá mór, mór uaim féin,

Agus ó na siúracha go léir,

Mise

Sr. Immaculata le Múire.

Present Community

Sr. Joan O'Regan
Sister Superior

Sr. Benignus Cremins

Sr. Mary Mooney
the most senior sister living in
St. Joseph's at present

Sr. Josephine Keohane
(transferred to Waterford
Nov. 2001)

Sr. Brendan Sheehy
keeps the Mercy tradition of
hospitality alive

Sr. De Lourdes Hegarty

Sr. Peter Ryan
one of the founding sisters of
the Florida mission

Sr. Immaculata Hourihane

Sr. Eleanor O'Leary

Sister Rosarii O'Shea *(picture not included)*

Sister Augustine Treacy *(picture not included)*

Sr. Kevin O'Brien

Sr. Catherine Linehan

Sr. Mary O'Donovan

Sr. Agnes Beary

Sr. Patricia Quinlan

Sr. Kieran O'Neill

Sr. Mary Oliver
'Novice mistress to so many of us'
McAuley House (Tralee)

Sr. Mary McAuliffe

Sr. Mary Anne Shannon,
(St Columbas, Cork)

List of deceased Sisters

Deceased members of the Community who will be left behind when the community moves to its new home.

From 1844 - 1913

The Sisters who witnessed the foundation take root, its growth, its extraordinary expansion, and who ministered to the people in times of poverty, hardships, famine Crimean War and diseases of various kinds.

	Name	Date	Comment
1.	Sr.M.Magdalen Murray	Nov. 20th 1852	
2.	Sr.M.Paul Murphy	March 17th 1853	
3.	Sr.M.Camillus Delahoyde	January 4th 1857	
4.	Sr.M.Camillus Brahan	February 19th 1860	
5.	Sr.M. Xavier O'Dwyer	January 1st 1862	
6.	Sr.M.Dominic O'Flynn	May 20th 1868	
7.	Mother Mary Anne Burke	March 22nd 1870	Foundress
8.	Mother M.Cecilia Mason	July 28th 1872	
9.	Sr.M.Agnes Burke	August 25th 1872	
10.	Sr.M.Brigid O'Brien	December 11th 1873	
11.	Sr.M.Augustine Carroll	June 15th 1875	
12.	Sr.M.Francis O'Flynn	March 8th 1877	
13.	Sr.M.Baptist Bridgeman	March 24th 1877	
14.	Sr.M. Columban Nolan	June 28th 1877	
15.	Sr.M.Columban Stokes	April 19th 1879	
16.	Sr.M.Ligouri O'Dwyer	May 3rd 1882	
17.	Mother M.Philomena Maher	February15th 1887	
18.	Mother M.Francis Bridgeman	February 11th 1888	First Superior - Crimea
19.	Sr.M.Vincent Dignam	October 17th 1890	
20.	Sr.M.Clare Keane	May 28th 1891	Crimea
21.	Sr.M.Alphonsus Reardon	April 23rd 1892	
22.	Sr.M.Evangelist O'Mahony	May 25th 1895	Member of Derby community who died in Dublin enroute to Kinsale
23.	Sr.M.Raphael Sexton	June 11th 1895	

24. Sr.M.Veronica Reardon	April 26th 1892	
25. M.M.Teresa Fallon	May 1st 1897	
26. Sr.M.Gonzaga Dunlea	March 26th 1898	
27. Sr.M.de Sales Kelly	July 19th 1898	
28. Sr.M.Camillus Darcy	March 9th 1899	
29. Sr.M.Genevieve Coghlan	October 20th 1902	
30. Sr.M.Benignus Scully	October 31st 1902	
31. M.M.Evangelist Fallon	June 27th 1903	
32. Sr.M.Brendan O'Brien	July 9th 1903	
33. Sr.M.Ita Colgan	December 1st 1903	
34. Sr.M.Michael O'Shea	August 15th 1904	
35. Sr.M.Magdalen Lordan	October 27th 1905	First to be buried in the new Cemetry
36. Sr.M.Borgia Hurley	August 3rd 1908	
37. Sr.M.de Pazzi Kilroe	February 23rd 1909	
38. Sr.M.Paul Egan	February 26th 1909	
39. Sr.M.Fachanan Murray	March 9th 1910	
40. Sr.M.Virgilius Barrett	June 22nd 1910	
41. Sr.M.Stanislaus Hurley	September 24th 1910	
42. Sr.M.Cecilia Moloney	October 26th 1910	
43. Sr.M.Elizabeth Martin	January 18th 1911	
44. Sr.M.Claver O'Hea	September 23rd 1912	
45. Sr.M.Brigid O'Dea	December 15th 1912	
46. Sr.M.Colmana Ellard	August 3rd 1913	

From 1914 – 1961

Sisters who witnessed World War 1, the Irish struggle, Civil War, Irish Independence, growth of Communism, World War 2, the influx of vocations and who took part in the great Missionary Movement.

47. Sr.M.Evangelist O'Connell	February 16th 1915
48. Sr.M.Philomena Cassin	August 15th 1915
49. Sr.M.Raphael Connolly	November 30th 1917
50. Sr.M.Scholastica Heffernan	January 7th 1918
51. Sr.M.Lorenza Mason	April 22nd 1918
52. Sr.M.Aquin Loughran	July 17th 1918
53. Sr.M.Baptist Mullally	December 18th 1918

54.	Sr.M.Albeus Coffey	August 17th 1919
55.	Sr.M.Rose Lynch	November 27th 1920
56.	Sr.M.Catherine Blake	May 13th 1921
57.	Sr.M.Gertrude O'Loughnan	September 27th 1921
58.	Sr.M.Joseph Hurley	May 14th 1923
59.	Sr.M.Bernard White	December 21st 1923
60.	Sr.M.Benignus O'Driscoll	January 19th 1925
61.	Sr.M.Canice Kelly	December 1st 1926
62.	Sr.M.Dominic Maloney	January 31st 1927
63.	Sr.M.Agatha Nunan	February 7th 1929
64.	Sr.M.Augustine Liston	March 19th 1929
65.	Sr.M.Bernardine Leahy	July 20th 1928
66.	Sr.M.Angela Barry	May 21st 1929
67.	Sr.M. Regis O'Brien	June 2nd 1930
68.	Sr.M.Peter Kelly	April 21st 1931
69.	Sr.M.Colmana Aherne	March 26th 1932
70.	Sr.M.Lelia Hogan	September 7th 1932
71.	Sr.M.Vincent Kenny	June 10th 1933
72.	Sr.M.Kevin Lawton	December 20th 1933
73.	Sr.M.Ursula Barry	November 27th 1935
74.	Sr.M.Josephine Doyle	August 31st 1937
75.	Sr.M. Alphonsus Quinn	June 23rd 1938
76.	Sr.M.Ita Thornton	February 15th 1939
77.	Sr.Mary O'Dwyer	June 6th 1939
78.	Sr.M.Eugenius Boyle	September 3rd 1939
79.	Sr.M.Columban Herbert	December 1st 1939
80.	M.M.Finbarr Carney	December 2nd 1939
81.	Sr.M.Columba Coakley	January 11th 1940
82.	M.M.Patrick Galvin	June 20th 1940
83.	Sr.M.Benedict Quinlan	August 2nd 1940
84.	Sr.M.Kieran O'Doherty	March 8th 1941
85.	Sr.M.Agnes Hayes	June 15th 1941
86.	Sr.M. Malachy Humphries	November 2nd 1942
87.	Sr.M.Brendan Stackpool	June 21st 1943
88.	Sr. M.Monica Twohig	March 30th 1944
89.	Sr.M.Thaddeus Quirke	July 10th 1944
90.	Sr.M.Magdalen Slattery	November 17th 1944

91. Sr.M.Ignatius O'Brien	July 14th 1945	
92. Sr.M.Clare Byron	August 22nd 1946	
93. Sr.M.Alacoque Reid	Janurary 1st 1947	
94. Sr.M.Bernadette Kennedy	April 3rd 1947	
95. Sr.M.Aloysius O'Gorman	March 14th 1951	
96. Sr.M.Xavier Keohane	May 30th 1951	
97. M.M.Aidan Hayes	November 27th 1953	
98. Sr.M.Francis Fitzgerald	December 1st 1953	
99. Sr.M.Berchmans Madigan	July 5th 1956	
100. Sr.M.de Sales Shelley	December 20th 1956	
101. Sr.M.Fintan Sheehan	July 12th 1957	
102. Sr.M.Veronica Barry	February 23rd 1958	
103. Sr.M.Gabriel Molougheny	March 3rd 1959	
104. Sr.M.Camillus Kiely	October 7th 1959	
105. Sr.M.Dympna Deasy	June 18th 1960	
106. Sr.M.Antonia Lynch	September 22nd 1961	

From 1962 - 2002

The Sisters who witnessed the period after Vatican Council 2, the changes in Religious Life that followed, rapid global changes, decline of vocations, the fall of the Berlin Wall, great advances in science and technology and the Celtic Tiger.

107. Sr.M.Brigid Lehane	November 26th 1962	
108. M.M.Teresa Kennedy	January 17th 1963	
109. Sr.M.de Pazzi Clay	August 8th 1965	
110. Sr.Catherine Costin	November 15th 1965	Postulant who had only been two weeks in the Convent.
111. Sr.M.Ethna Crowe	August 24th 1966	
112. Sr.M.Agatha Gurhy	June 15th 1969	
113. Sr.M.Virgilius Fingleton	January 10th 1970	
114. Sr.M.Stanislaus Lyons	November 28th 1970	
115. Sr.M.Philomena Smyth	April 6th 1971	
116. M.M.Enda Costelloe	April 12th 1971	
117. Sr.M.Michael Slattery	May 27th 1972	
118. Sr.M.Canice Power	May 5th 1975	
119. Sr.M.Raphael O.Sullivan	May 12th 1980	
120. Sr.M.Lawrence O'Neill	October 1st 1982	

121. Sr.M.Evangelist O'Brien	March 16th 1984
122. Sr.M.Aquin Mulvey	March 14th 1985
123. Sr.M.Cecilia O'Flynn	January 19th 1986
124. Sr.M.Regina Sheehan	September 1st 1987
125. Sr.M.Bernard Millett	September 6th 1992
126. Sr.M.Emmanuel Lynch	September 18th 1994
127. Sr.M.Rose Carroll	February 16th 1995
128. Sr.M.Imelda O'Grady	May 1st 1995
129. Sr.M.Baptist Molloy	May 19th 1996
130. Sr.M.Kevin Ryan	August 11th 1997
131. Sr.M.Columba Gallagher	April 8th 1998
132. Sr.M.Angela Kelly	October 4th 1999
133. Sr.Maureen Ryan	November 18th 1999
134. Sr.M.Albert Treacy	April 14th 2000
135. Sr.M.Carmel Meany	April 11th 2001
136. Sr. Fachtnan Sheehan	October 23rd 2001

Bibliography

Archives: Convent of Mercy, Kinsale

Frank Hurley 1994 *St.Joseph's Convent of Mercy, Kinsale*

Sr.M.Bertrand Degnan R.S.M, *Mercy Unto Thousands*, 1957

Sr.Mary Aurelia McArdle *California's Pioneer Sister of Mercy - Mother Baptist Russell (1829 - 1898)*

Mother Austin Carroll: *Leaves from the Annals of the Sisters of Mercy Volumes 1 - 4.*

Father Matthew Russell S.J. 1912, *The Three Sisters of Lord Russell*

Sr.Rose McArdle *Mercy Undaunted - 125 years in California*

Sr.Angela Bolster 1964 *The Sisters of Mercy in the Crimean War*; Mercer Press

Mary Ellen Evans 1959 *The Spirit is Mercy, The Sisters of Mercy in the Archdiocese of Cincinnati 1858 - 1958*; Newman Press

Michael Mulcahy B.E. 1966 *A Short History of Kinsale*

Sr.M.Joseph Kelly. *St.Catherine's Convent, Ballyshannon 1867 - 1994*

Sr.Mary Lucy McDonald 1981 *By Her Fruits - The story of Sr.Joseph Lynch.*

Sr.Margaret Molitor - Archivist of the Cincinnati Region - September 1993.*The Biography of Sister Mary Teresa Maher*

Sister Barbara Jeffrey: *Sisters of Mercy Derby 1849 - 1999 - A Sesquicentennial Celebration.*

Brendan Doyle: *Meditations with Julian of Norwich*; Bear & Co.

Matthew Fox: *Meditations with Meister Eckhart*; Bear & Co.

Bede Griffiths *The Marriage of East and West*; Fount

Joan Chittister O.S.B. 1997 *The Fire in These Ashes - A Spirituality of Contemporary Religious Life*; Racewing Press.

Mary McAleese: *Reconciled Being - Love in Chaos - The John Main Seminar* 1997; Medio Media

Paramahansa Yogananda. *Where There is Light - Insight and Inspiration for Meeting Life's Challenges*

Thomas Berry 1988 - *The Dream of the Earth*

John O'Donoghue, *Anam Cara* 1997; Bantam Press

Misericordia

The Mercy Shield

1. THE CROWN BEARING THE MONOGRAM
   (a) The Patroness of the Mercy Institute, the Mother of Mercy who is a Queen. The monogram means MARIA REGINA.
   (b) It is a reminder of the RULE: "The sisters shall endeavour to inspire the children with a sincere devotion to the Immaculate Mother of God." And also of the injunction of our Foundress: "We ought to give proof of our love for Our Blessed Lady by imitating her, and trying to make all under our care imitate her also."

2. THE SEVEN BARS
   (a) The seven spiritual and corporal works of Mercy, the Mercy Apostolate proper.
   In the colour scheme for these bars, some history is implied. Four of them are red and three green; they are arranged alternately. The four red ones are taken from the flag of King James of Aragon, who had been a joint founder of the mediaeval Order of Ransom or Mercy, for the redemption of captives with St. Peter Nolasco. To the newly founded Order the King granted the privilege of adopting his ensign as its special badge. It was from this mediaeval Order of Mercy that Mother McAuley got the distinguishing title for her modern Institute.
   The three Green Bars represent three extra vows to serve the Poor, Sick and Ignorant, taken by all Sisters of Mercy.
   (b) These seven bars signify also, the seven gifts of the Holy Spirit.

3. THE CELTIC CROSS
   (a) The Irish origin of the Sisters of Mercy.
   (b) From the point of view of salvation, it combines the symbol of Redemption and of the Sacred Passion with that of the Holy Eucharist.

4. THE ANCHOR
   Testifies to Mother McAuley's unwavering faith and confidence in God.

5. THE MOTTO
   MISERICORDIA. Mother McAuley meant the word MERCY to designate the spirit of her Institute.

THE SHIELD IN COLOUR

Crown: Gold; Monogram, blue.	*Celtic Cross:* Gold, on a blue field.
Bars: Red, green, on a gold field.	*Anchor:* Gold on a green field.
Scroll: Gold; Misericordia, blue.	*Outline:* Red, to suggest "the bond of charity".

MOTHER McAULEY'S LEGACY TO HER ORDER